Begin Where You Are

Begin Where You Are

Messages of Meaning

BETTY BLAND

Published in 2023 by Bedford Books
2040 Hornbeck Court
Raleigh, NC 27614

Compilation copyright © 2023 by Betty Bland
Foreword copyright © 2023 by Tim Boyd

Design and production by Drew Stevens

COVER IMAGE:
Tourist on a Summer Day by Suzanne Hetzel
dragonflywatercolors.com
© 2021 by Suzanne Hetzel

Image of the author on page ii © by Tim Boyd

This book is dedicated to my dear friend and colleague, Tim Boyd. We first met in the early 1970s as fellow seekers at the Theosophical Society in America (TSA), in Wheaton, Illinois. Through our mutual work for the TSA, we developed the bonds of a deep friendship based on a shared purpose and mutual appreciation. Tim served as my vice president while I was president of the TSA and succeeded me as National President. He is currently the International President of the Theosophical Society at Adyar in Chennai, India. Upon my retirement, Tim presented me with a small volume of my writings along with a number of personal pictures. Tim, you got this ball rolling a number of years ago. Many thanks to you for everything.

CONTENTS

FOREWORD

I CANNOT SAY precisely when I first met Betty. I do know that it was at least 45 years ago. I have photos from around that time. For more than 30 of those years, we worked closely together at the Theosophical Society in America: first locally, then as National Directors, later as Vice President, and then as President of the TSA. In each of those positions, I followed in her wake.

Four decades of acquaintance can tell you a lot about a person. Four decades of close involvement in often difficult, demanding, and uncertain circumstances tells more. Martin Luther King, Jr. made this observation: "The ultimate measure of a man is not where he stands in moments of comfort and convenience, but where he stands at times of challenge and controversy." Having been with Betty through both ease and turmoil, I consider myself a competent judge of who and what she is.

The importance of the teacher is recognized in spiritual traditions around the world. In Tibetan Buddhism, the role of the teacher in drawing out the deeper regions of consciousness is referred to as the "foundation of all perfections" -- a necessity in the life of the aspiring individual. A person of genuine understanding is especially important for those just awakening to their deeper potential. For most, the ultimate direction of their searching is clear, but the road leading there is not. Particularly in the beginning stages of a spiritual path, a small step in the wrong direction, continued over time, leads people far from their desired goal. This is when advice from a qualified spiritual friend is invaluable. For many of us that "friend" comes in the form of a book. It is a feature of the spiritual endeavor that all information and ideas are not equal. Words repeated by someone lacking in personal transformative experience, though true, cannot carry the motivating energy of those same words from one who has lived them.

Betty took on the mantle of leadership for an organization whose motto is, "There is no religion higher than Truth." In doing so, she set a high bar for herself. Education, philosophy, organizational skill, and opinions alone do not suffice. The difficulty with Truth of the deeper sort is that one's relationship to it reveals itself less in words spoken than in the life one lives. The qualities of unforced kindness, compassion, friendliness, honesty, patience, courage, and humor are the markings of someone rooted in what is real. It has been said that "who you are speaks so loudly, I can't hear a word you are saying." This is not to say that the spoken or written word is without power. The words of one who has done the long and arduous work of cultivating the hidden powers of the heart are imbued with power and authority. This book is an example. Written with clarity and simplicity, it illuminates the essentials of a genuine spiritual life.

Often it takes crisis to focus our attention, but in whatever phase of life we find ourselves there is always the possibility for a new beginning. Although too often shrouded in complexity, there is a simple truth at the core of the spiritual life. Saint Francis stated it thus: "What you are looking for, is what is looking." Within each of us there is something -- a seed, a presence -- and when we finally sense it, it leads us on our spiritual path. There is no missing "something" that we need to find and add to ourselves in order to be whole. It is not a person, place, or practice we are lacking. Writing about Grace, which she describes as "unmerited divine assistance," Betty says, "Grace is not something to be received, but something inside each of us to be discovered." It could not be said better. Begin where you are.

—Tim Boyd, International President of the
Theosophical Society, Adyar

PREFACE

HOW DOES ONE wake up to a spiritual quest? Sometimes it comes from a sudden realization and sometimes more gradually from a growing understanding of life's experiences. My particular "wake-up call" came suddenly as a result of a Near-Death Experience (NDE) in 1968, well before that became a mainstream term. The NDE catapulted me on a search to understand my experience and to put that knowledge into practice.

Fortunately, early in my search I encountered the Theosophical Society in America (TSA) which provided a wealth of helpful information. Its comprehensive worldview provided a roadmap for the continuing exploration that became my life's path and ever-unfolding growth. The joy and sense of fulfillment in following this new path led me to many areas of service within the TSA and ultimately to my accepting the role of National President. As President, I had the opportunity to share with the readers of *Quest* magazine what walking that path had taught me.

Over my 9-year term I delighted in sharing the wisdom I was so blessed to discover in the Viewpoint column of the regularly published *Quest* magazine. Over time I learned that my words resonated with many readers. After urgings from a number of people, I finally decided to make these articles more readily available. This collection of reflections offers threads of thought to inspire a deeper awareness of the meaning and purpose of our time on this earth and our calling to act responsibly for the well-being of all our fellow beings.

I offer this publication in the hope that as you read, you will find something that helps you connect to the beauty and inter-wovenness of our amazing creation—that it might in some way make your life more meaningful.

My warmest wishes for a joy-filled journey,

Betty Bland

Begin Where You Are

A MORNING WALK

WHERE DOES ONE start when facing a new and difficult problem? We have heard, "one step at a time." I would modify that to "many steps," in the form of a morning walk. Now, I admit that most folks would not want to walk as fast as is my practice, but everyone would profit from participating in the grand awakening of nature that occurs every morning. The returning sun brings fresh energy and sparkle to green and growing things, rain or shine, just as our returning consciousness, after a night of rest or a moment of meditation, glistens with renewal from other realms.

For me, moving into the role of president-administrator of the Theosophical Society in America presents an exciting and multifaceted challenge. Issues concerning publishing, programs, personnel, finances, library, membership, public outreach, facility management, educational effort, and community living swirl around as an ever-productive, many-headed hydra, beneficial, but complex in nature. The real task, however, is to view all of this with morning-fresh eyes to assure that the swirl is ever new and creative in accomplishing its valuable purposes.

The swirl of concerns and responsibilities that everyone has, sometimes a rapid whirlpool, sometimes a gentle eddy, needs to be viewed with fresh understanding daily. It is all too easy to lose sight of the garden, for being focused on the weeds. And what is

1

a weed, but a plant out of place? There is a solution embedded within every problem; there is an opportunity within every crisis. The operative advice here is, "TRY."

Several years ago when I was talking about my approaching presidency with Radha Burnier, our international president, she acknowledged the responsibility one bears as designated guardian and guide for the Society. There are always difficulties, compromising situations, and less than perfect people. (Surely not!) "Yet," she said, "if one does one's best both in action and in maintaining the inner focus, then help will come if needed and asked for." None of us is alone; our higher selves and all the forces for good—the power that many call God—are available to magnify our own feeble efforts. Help will come; we just have to do our part.

On a morning walk recently after a rain shower, there was, wiggling frantically on the pavement in front of me, a fat, slimy earthworm trying to make its way to higher dryer ground, but stuck and getting nowhere fast. Its activity caught my eye and generated pity for its plight. There was no doubt that this was a lively worm, full of spunk, and well deserving of a rescue pause. Putting on my brakes and wrinkling up my nose, I gingerly scooped up this slippery denizen of the earth and deposited it in the grass. As it slipped gratefully into its natural abode, I was struck by the comparison. If it had "thrown up its little hands," and given up all effort, then it would never have experienced the miracle of being lifted up over the insurmountable barrier of the sidewalk. The secret is to keep wiggling.

How to solve any problem involves taking that first step, but it also means taking innumerable steps, becoming a walk, as the footprint becomes the path. And our life pathway that runs through the "pathless land" of existence requires a dewdrop-like freshness of vision if the way is to be found, and a patiently enduring effort if we would have help along the way.

CLIMBING TREES AND INITIATIONS

I RECENTLY WATCHED a man trimming tree limbs that overhang power lines. He works for the power company as the foreman of an off-road crew of workers who climb trees in wilderness areas where trucks cannot go. It is an amazing sight to see a grown man run up the side of a tree as if he were running up the stairs in his own home. What would seem an impossible task is not so hard when one has the right strength, skills, and tools such as shoe spikes, safety belt, and ropes and pulleys—besides, of course, the requisite power saw hanging from his belt.

I commented to him about his skill, and he replied that he was just getting really good at it. He has climbed trees this way for twenty years, twenty to twenty-five trees a day, five days a week. The performance that looked so easy became so only because of much hard work. He was not so skilled at first, but developed his prowess over time.

Time is that universal commodity that carries us along our path. As this new year edges into our awareness, we note its entrance and naturally reflect on beginnings. Every beginning is an ending of something old as well as the commencement of something new. A beginning is a kind of initiation, one among the many that we experience in a lifetime.

Some initiations are a function of time, such as our passage from youth to adulthood, and again into middle age and old age. Other initiations are a result of our successfully traversing the gauntlets that life presents to us. In fact, if we have committed ourselves to the spiritual path, life is one long series of initiations. Every trial and every problem to be solved are chances to learn and opportunities to pass the test. If we fail, we can be sure the problem will arise again in a new way, against which we can struggle and strengthen our ability to finally overcome. Somewhere among the daily lessons, we gain insight so that what might have seemed insurmountable becomes merely a pebble on the way.

Some people think that spiritual initiations can be bought and sold, or at least bestowed on believers through incantations or rituals. This is a ridiculous pandering to our prideful nature. The credulous want to know the exact number of initiations they have passed and their own level of attainment—to put them a notch above others. Not long ago someone told me that this life was the last time they would have to be born into this world, having already achieved the fourth initiation. I was impressed at how far advanced they indeed must be—and yet I saw them struggling with the same kinds of issues that dislodge my own self-installed halo.

Chutzpah of this kind afflicted some members of the Theosophical Society in the early decades of the last century. Unfortunately a number of new aspirants were so excited about the ideal of human progression and perfection that they became carried away with their own self-importance. Such hubris, among other things, prompted the adepts to command that this "cant of the masters" must be put down. Today I hope that we have reached a level of maturity that will help us avoid that pitfall.

Why should I mention a tree-climber at the beginning of a discussion about initiations? Like the tree-climber, we have to work to develop our strengths, which are developed only through concerted effort. Life skills, spiritual will, and the critical tool of ego-less wisdom are not imposed on us from outside. They are hard won through serious introspection, mindful living, and acts of kindness. We have to do our homework.

There may be certain events, influences, or people that catapult us into setting our evolutionary course, but it is the self-induced and self-devised efforts of each soul on its obligatory pilgrimage (as H. P. Blavatsky indicates in the third fundamental proposition of *The Secret Doctrine*) that finally win the prize.

The razor-sharp abilities required to become an adept, a super-human on the higher rungs of the evolutionary ladder, are not easily gained, nor do they puff up one's own self-importance. Rather, they bring us through the wilderness to the treetop—to the ultimate goal of service:

> There is a road, steep and thorny, beset with perils of every kind, but yet a road, and it leads to the very heart of the Universe: I can tell you how to find those who will show you the secret gateway that opens inward only, and closes fast behind the neophyte for evermore. There is no danger that dauntless courage cannot conquer; there is no trial that spotless purity cannot pass through; there is no difficulty that strong intellect cannot surmount. For those who win onwards there is reward past all telling—the power to bless and save humanity . . . ." (HPB, *Collected Writings* 13:219)

As we move along in this new year, let us hone our skills for the service of others. Let us make this a year of true initiation.

EXCESSIVE HAPPINESS

To be free is to be happy without seeking happiness,
to act with a spontaneous motion which is the resultant of an inward grace.
                    —N. Sri Ram, *Thoughts for Aspirants*

IN THE MOVIE *Patch Adams*, based on actual events, Patch, a medi-
cal student, is almost expelled from school because he is guilty of
"excessive happiness." When one is dealing with life and death
matters, one must be serious. And yet the patients with whom he
cavorts respond better to treatment and are generally happier and
more cooperative because they are treated as unique individuals
and because they can laugh—even in the midst of suffering. Humor
has broken the clouds of despair and let the sunshine of grace pour
in. The patients did nothing but become open to that grace. And
their laughter created the opening for it to enter their lives.

   Grace is a great thing to have, but how does one work for it? Or
even put oneself in the firing line of grace, when by its very definition it is unmerited divine assistance? How can one earn something
that is not earnable?

   The secret is that grace is not something to be received, but
something inside each of us to be discovered. Every living person

has a seed of grace planted within, a seed that will sprout and come into full flower with care and feeding.

What can we feed this mysterious little seed? We want to force-feed it, to check every few days to see if it has grown yet. But attention is one of the things that smother it. Grace can only grow when left alone. What a dilemma! We can't force it; we can't control it; but we can become open to that which is all around and within us. We can let it happen.

I have already given one hint about how this might be so by mentioning that humor supports grace. A good belly laugh a day can surely keep the doctor away. Yet there are several additional ways to cultivate that illusive lily of life—namely, silence, thankfulness, and service.

First consider silence. In the silence is a profound stillness that gives rise to deep connections with the source of all life and joy. As it says in the Bible, "Be still and know that I am God." Under the gentle blanket of silence, our seed of grace sends down strong roots and shoots upward toward the sun. Yet, keeping silent can be a difficult task.

A friend recently confessed that she had no luck in meditating. Thoughts were always popping into her head, and she couldn't keep from fidgeting. She supposed that it was just beyond her. "But," she said, "I breathe little prayers of thanksgiving all day long. Every day I see the many good things and joys in life that far outweigh the bad, and I say a little thank-you."

You can be sure that I told her that breathing "little prayers of thanksgiving" is one of the most powerful meditations one can do. With this kind of prayerful attitude, the opening to joy is a natural outgrowth. Frequent acknowledgment that life and everything that comes with it are a gift, brings to us the treasure of a richer life—through grace.

If one has had any success at all with humor, silence, and thankfulness, then the conditions will be right for grace to flower in all of its splendor. The petals will unfold naturally in an outward-turned attitude of service. Such service does not necessarily involve intense activity, as one might have expected, although it may. It may just occur in very quiet ways, depending on one's circumstances. Universally, however, it incorporates a gentle sharing of oneself in the calm assurance that all will be well:

> When all life becomes a poem of service, in the true, pure, inward sense, then all life grows exceedingly beautiful; it unfolds like a flower. (N. Sri Ram, *Thoughts for Aspirants*)

May the grace of excessive happiness bloom in your heart.

THE GAME OF LIFE

UNCERTAINTY IS ONE of the greatest obstacles with which we human beings have to contend. Indeed, as I write this, war is raging in Iraq, with no certainty of outcome and with pain on every side. Such imminent danger increases the difficulty of dealing with the unpredictable. So perhaps it is useful to explore how we might cope with uncertainty.

For those who enjoy sports contests and even for those who enjoy playing games of various sorts, part of the enjoyment is the edge of not knowing who will win. The contest keeps us fascinated—just like a good mystery story in which we try to outguess the creative genius of the author. In these cases we consider the excitement pleasurable because the stakes are not so high-although some sports fans seem to lose sight of that fact.

But if the outcome of the game affects us personally, then our anxiety level rises. This is one of the reasons that Tiger Woods has become such a folk hero. When his income and his reputation are riding on a single golf swing, he can often achieve a meditative calmness that allows him to perform to perfection. And even at those times when he is off his game, he still seems to maintain a degree of coolness envied by most golfers. He has a certain assurance, as if he realizes that indeed it is only a game.

The stakes grow even higher when our own safety is at risk, or the safety of loved ones, or of our country, or even our way of life. And yet, if we believe the Theosophical ideas of karma and the Divine Plan, then all of life is a kind of game, as our inner essence (or higher self) wends its way on the pilgrim journey of return to our source. Although blindfolded by our attachments to the illusory nature of the world, we have an opportunity to gain understanding and develop skills that move us along on our path. Even in the thick of things, where discomfort is high, we are in the right situation through which we can grow. If we can open our vision wide enough, we may be able to see that the situation was chosen for us by our higher Self (not by our ease-seeking personality) as a chance to learn.

Whenever we find ourselves in trying circumstances, we can realize that we have been presented with an opportunity. We are being tested and trained to strengthen our resolve and to focus solely on our spiritual essence—our one true Self. In her small book Practical Occultism, Madam Blavatsky wrote:

> The "God" in us—that is to say, the Spirit of Love and Truth, Justice and Wisdom, Goodness and Power—should be our only true and permanent *Love*, our only reliance in everything, our only *Faith*, which, standing firm as a rock, can for ever be trusted; our only *Hope*, which *will* never fail us if all other things perish.

For most of us, this spiritual essence may seem impossible to reach, but it is attainable and worth all the effort it takes. To seek it, we have to begin where we are. All life is our classroom; our friends and enemies alike are our teachers; books and fellow student-pilgrims support our study. Seeking this inner knowing with an open heart will bring us into contact with the mentors we need.

Perhaps a good beginning, in addition to daily meditation, would be to try regularly to remember who we truly are. When we are so reminded, we can better play the game of life and walk with certainty in the face of uncertainty. A helpful practice is to use bells as signals to recall us to our origins and reason for being. Whenever a bell sounds—a distant chime, a clock, or even an inner ringing, repeat quietly the saying from the Buddhist contemplative tradition: "Listen, listen, listen to the wondrous sound of the bell. It calls me back to my one true Self."

Whatever troubles are in the outer world, within that Self in each of us is a calm assurance. Whenever we access that center of certainty, endurance, and peace, we make it more available to both ourselves and others. May we all find that peace and may it abide in all beings. Shanti.

THE ZEN OF WATER SKIING

WATER SKIING IS one of those sports that requires a good sense of balance that cannot be based on any exterior prop. The constant motion of the water gives no reliable foundation, and although the rope is pulling the skier, the skier cannot pull on the rope. A novice skier can have plenty of frustration until learning to rely on the center balance point. As any good skier knows, one must maintain an interior balance somewhere just below the solar plexus, somewhat akin to the balance of a gyroscope. From this balance point, the shock of the waves can be absorbed with flexing knees and the pull of the rope can be equalized.

One's relationship to life in many ways resembles the skier's relationship to rope and water. In life, we are buffeted by troubled waters—emotional and circumstantial. We are catapulted forward by time and pushed back by our own limitations. Dealing with these difficulties gracefully would seem an impossible task were it not for the knowledge that there is a reliable center which is unaffected by the turbulence. Somewhere deep inside each one of us is the divine spark, the inner self, which partakes of the divine universals—power of presence, reliable awareness, and eternal bliss (Sat, Chit, and Ananda). We may not consciously identify these attributes of our center of being, but life's ups and downs can teach us that this interior self is ultimately the only true point of reference.

As we seek to expand our contact with that center, its realities become more clear.

In her forward to *Doctrine of the Heart*, Annie Besant speaks of the need to balance opposites for the spiritually attuned life. On the one hand we as aspirants are told to be without desire, without passion, unmoved by the vicissitudes of life. Yet on the other hand we are constantly exhorted to feel the anguish of every suffering creature as if it were our own. One should be uninvolved, and at the same time deeply involved. In other words it is necessary to operate from that balance point which can only be found in the eternal unitive Self.

A similar dilemma appears in the little spiritual guidebook written by Krishnamurti as a young boy, *At the Feet of the Master*. Of the four qualifications given for the spiritual life, the second is desirelessness. This is the qualification of desirelessness. The aspirant is to have no care for comforts, powers, cleverness, or even approbations, and should stay out of other people's business. Yet, this part culminates with an exhortation to come to the rescue of the weak and downtrodden. The booklet ends with the fourth qualification, which is love. (The other two are discrimination and right conduct.) In the second qualification, the aspirant is encouraged to care less; in the fourth, the aspirant is told to care more. Here again we see the importance of finding that calm balance point called equanimity.

In Buddhism the "Four Immeasurables" for the spiritual life are catalogued as the wish for all beings to be happy, the wish for the suffering of all beings to cease, delight in the good fortune of others, and equanimity. Once more there is the exhortation to be immersed in the world while at the same time remaining balanced and away from the fray of the madding crowd.

The only way we can achieve this balance is to strengthen

awareness of that center point of peace within, through meditation and self-study, identifying with the One Reality—the ground of being. If we truly touch that center, then we can maintain our equilibrium even in the face of death, pain, and loss. We can trust that this physical life, maya, or illusory existence, has a reality and purpose that is far deeper and more profound than it appears surface. When we finally learn this lesson, we will be able to ride life's waves without falling into the sea; we will be able to endure the pulls and tugs while yet remaining centered in peace. We will know how to live.

> Before the eyes can see,
>   They must be incapable of tears
> Before the ear can hear,
>   It must have lost its sensitiveness
> Before the voice can speak in the presence of the Masters
>   It must have lost the power to wound
> Before the soul can stand in the presence of the Masters
>   Its feet must be washed in the blood of the heart.
>   *Light on the Path*

PAYING ATTENTION

MOST OF US have heard about the formation of a pearl in an oyster by an irritant such as a grain of sand. From this example, an analogy is often drawn for our own lives, in which the traumas of life can be the irritants that bring about the formation of the pearls of spirit within our own beings.

The pain and suffering of life, or *dukka*, as mentioned in Buddhist teachings, is not a favorite subject. We don't like to think of what Shakespeare called the "uses of adversity" (in *Midsummer Night's Dream*) until we find ourselves in a painful situation. Then, as we cast about for rhyme or reason, we might use the pearl analogy to find some comfort. ("This medicine tastes so terrible it is bound to be good for me.") More often, however, we tend to use this analogy when comforting others rather than applying such insight to our own difficulties.

Ah, there's the rub. It is no fun to sit with the pain with full attention; yet sitting with the problem, paying close attention to the experience and its associations with our past is the necessary elixir. When we have problems, we might do any of several things. We can pretend there is nothing wrong, but by doing so we shut out our awareness, creating a reservoir of unrecognized anguish that either explodes in our relationships with others or results in the inward implosion of depression. Or instead of blocking, we can end up obsessing over the situation, continuously rehashing and strengthening its hold on ourselves.

One of the heart's first impulses is to clamp tightly shut against the irritation. Defensive walls go up; offensive, prickly behavior blocks out all who might support us emotionally or be a mirror through which we might gain insight. Like an earthworm reacting to a salty fingertip, the heart retreats quickly into its recesses of heavy darkness rather than facing the possibility of being brought out into the light of conscious attention. Now, for an earthworm that is a healthy fight/flight reflex, but for us two-leggeds of complex psychological nature, whose souls long for the sun, it is a tragic reaction resulting in a continuation of pain and counterproductive behavior.

An essential element in our spiritual growth is finding a way to open the shell around our hearts—but not just any opening. The trick is to open to the light of intuition—through calm, dispassionate observation, rather than staying caught in the whirlwind of our emotional reactions. In this process we have to be careful to look with a quietly intuitive perception that allows us to see things as they really are. All too often we might mistakenly view our remembering, rehashing, and reminding others as attempts to open ourselves to clarity and awareness. But these patterns are the very substance of the tightly shut shell within which we go around and around, thinking we must be making progress.

Equally imprisoning is the pretense that there is no pain and no shell. We can say, grimacing through gritted teeth, "Everything is rosy. Can't you see me smiling?" Very often we might not realize what this line of defense does to ourselves and to others. We might even feel quite proud of ourselves that we are such cheerful martyrs! Yet this tactic not only locks that shell down tightly, it also makes that carefully crafted shell invisible to ourselves so that we are oblivious to the hurt our reactions inflicted on others.

Have you ever had a bad day that you just wanted to be able to discuss with a friend? You didn't want them to climb mountains or slay dragons for you, but you just wanted them to pay attention to you with a sympathetic ear. In so doing, they were actually supporting you as you began processing the event and its implications in your life.

Although it is as familiar as our breathing, consciousness has many complexities. The ordinary waking consciousness in which most of us function is the level where the irritations begin and continue to grow. On the other hand, at a deeper level of our consciousness resides the watcher within, our inner or higher self. This is the level of the attention payer, the healer, the pearl maker.

The only way to open our shell is to relax our tight grip and allow it to open from within. Instead of running from the difficulty, or continuously inflicting grief upon ourselves and others, we can stop, take a deep breath, and say to ourselves, "There must be a better way." In that moment of inquiry lies the beginning of hope. Something from the depths of our being, which has been watching and waiting all along, responds with hope and assurance. At first it is only a glimmer, but with attention it will grow. Focused awareness can ferret out those seeds of distress and heal them with clear insight.

Little by little we can learn to trust the presence of this light as we walk through the inevitable difficulties. We don't have to shut ourselves tightly up, obsessively repeat the scenario, or pretend that nothing is wrong. We can look into the difficulties until they yield a great blessing of insight. Through every difficulty we can find a tool or key that will enable us to open the door to the deeper parts of ourselves where our true nature, a reflection of the divine, abides.

As it is said in the little spiritual guidebook *At The Feet Of The Master*, written by Krishnamurti when he was quite young:

> You must trust yourself. You say you know yourself too well? If you feel so, you do not know yourself; you only know the weak outer husk, which has fallen often into the mire. But you—the real you—you are a spark of God's own fire, and God, who is Almighty, is in you, and because of that there is nothing that you cannot do if you will. (55)

With this kind of confidence, we are able to relax our anxious minds and doubting hearts enough to allow our shells of defense to begin to open, and then to fall away altogether. The source of healing was there all along and it was only our own insecurity that kept our consciousness shut too tightly to find it. Focused awareness will gradually transform our world and our perceptions of it into an iridescent beauty. Because we dare to face a problem rather than close it out, our insight can create understanding and compassion. Our discomfort will become a pearl of blessing.

May our pearls shine for the benefit of all.

LETTING GO TO RECEIVE

IT MAY BE a simple thing for those who do not have the same fixed Taurus nature that I have, but for me moving is the most odious task of a lifetime—and I ought to know since I have made many major moves. While I am writing this there are boxes and chaos all around me. The upheaval calls to mind the importance of being able to let go.

First there is the issue of selling the house. It is difficult to guess how this ordeal will proceed. The right buyer has to be found. Price and timing have to work. But there is also an inner side to the process. When we moved from Kentucky where our children had grown up, I was most reluctant to leave. I said I was ready to go, and I made all the right efforts, but my heart of hearts was just not in it. Part of me was still clinging to our home and garden spot, which we had built and created for ourselves. It took us a full year to sell that house. Reflecting back on it, I realize that my unwillingness to let go actually created an inhibiting energy. I was unconsciously blocking the process.

There is a tradition that if one cannot sell a house, a statue of St. Joseph should be buried upside down in the back yard. In fact rumor has it that in some areas where this tradition is strong, one can tell how many times a house has been sold just by digging up the back yard and seeing how many St. Joseph statues there are.

A realtor friend of mine told me that she had to replace the Joseph in her nativity set several times before she bought some cheap St. Joseph statues and began retrieving them from the back yard of a house after it had been sold.

We do not know a whole lot about Joseph, the carpenter and earthly father of Jesus, except that he was obedient to God and a dutiful husband. Perhaps as the model householder, he is the guardian of a stable home. By burying him upside down, one might break that pattern of stability and be free to move on.

I thought about that recently when we were trying to sell the house in Pennsylvania. I had delayed jumping into the real estate market all spring, until I realized I was holding a resistant attitude. After a good talking to myself, my release was sufficient enough to effect a quick sale. Thereafter, however, I was confronted further with the tearing down and packing up process—another letting go. Life is the great teacher and will continually provide these little lessons until we get it. In every area of life we need to be able to let go of old circumstances in order to make way for the new. This not-so-easy discipline is a cornerstone for the spiritual life. The second Fundamental Proposition of the Secret Doctrine says that there is a constant movement, a cyclicity of all forces in nature. If our lives, as part of that flux, are in a continuous state of change, then one of the most painful things we can do for ourselves is to try to hold on to things as unchangeable, in avoidance of the inevitable. We have to be able to let go of possessions, habits, and patterns, as we encounter change from moment to moment.

An aspiring student had the privilege of being invited by a Zen master to a tea ceremony. The anxious would-be student put on fine clothing and best manners for the auspicious occasion. After properly performing the ritual, the master asked the student to hold out the cup. The master carefully poured the cup full, and then kept pouring and pouring until the cup ran over into the saucer and spilled over onto the floor. In response to the student's puzzled inquiry, the master said, "It is clear that a full cup cannot be a vessel for more tea, just as a mind that is full of its own self-importance cannot receive new teachings. When you have digested what you know, and are an empty vessel, come back and I will pour out for you new understanding."

Many areas of our lives can benefit from an attitude of greater openness. On the physical level we might be more ready to move, or relinquish cherished possessions. On the emotional level we might cling less tightly to the compulsion to have things our way, to be the center of attention and adulation, or to be so possessive of loved ones. On the mental level, we might be able to recognize our most precious ideas as tentative hypotheses open to expanded horizons of understanding. And on the deepest levels of spirit we can be open to the wonder and magic of consciousness, especially as it reveals to us our unity with all of life. This kind of openness is a gift that enfolds us and those we encounter within a universal atmosphere of loving-kindness.

So I suggest that we all perform the imaginary ritual of burying St. Joseph in our mental back yards as a way of committing to being more open to the many gifts of life. We can let go of our prized possessions and attachments in order to receive the greatest gift of all—love.

PATTERNS OF LIGHT AND DARK

THIS IS A particularly good time to view patterns of light and dark. At this time of year nature's palette becomes very limited, and shadows stand out in stark relief against a pale backdrop. Similarly in black and white photography, the lack of diversity of color brings a sharper focus to the patterns and textures that are there all along, but camouflaged by a variety of bright diversions. Since winter is traditionally known as a time for introspection and reflection, it seems appropriate to consider the patterns—those in the world around us and those within our minds.

The shapes created by trees as they stretch their bony fingers across the winter sky have always fascinated me. In fact this is true in every season—the feathery tips of spring, the rich density and herringbones of summer, and the ever-sparser shapes as leaves whirl away in the fall. In each of these instances, the additional essential element of the pattern is the light beyond—the backdrop of either a gray, or blue, or sparkling sky against which these shapes can display their character. In order to see the full beauty of the pattern, one's focus can neither be on the nearer branch, nor on the light behind, but on the two in their interactions with each other.

This same idea can be applied to the understanding of our life experiences. Whatever is happening now, whatever memories we carry, or whatever paradigms we hold through which we view our world, each can only begin to have meaningful form or pattern when viewed against the backdrop of spiritual insight. When seen in this light, patterns emerge which yield meaning and healing; the luminosity of understanding and compassion become an intrinsic part of the pattern.

In his translation and exposition of Patanjali's *Yoga Sutras* (*The Science of Yoga*), Taimni refers to the essential yogic technique of quieting the *vrittis* of our minds. He explains this Sanskrit term as referring to the functions or modifications of the mind. Although this technical term in yoga may seem far afield from our current discussion, it is not. Our individual minds habitually function along pathways that form a prison house around our consciousness. The Yoga Sutras tell us that those prison bars are structured by the way we think and act in response to life's predicaments. We are formed by the patterns we create and maintain through our attitudes, decisions, and actions. We may think the world is doing "it" to us, but in fact we are doing "it" to ourselves. We are forming the prison that conforms us.

Several of the Christian traditions use the term "formation" to describe their indoctrination classes for new members, in recognition of the need to re-form attitudes and outlook on life. The classes teach neophytes how to view life "in terms of God's laws so that they can learn to live a new life in Christ." The same principle applies here. One needs to be able to apply the light of spiritual understanding in order to be able to see the overall pattern, and seeing the greater pattern, attune one's life to be in closer harmony with it. Each action thus adjusted provides further clarity for more effective understanding and more harmonious living. And so the virtuous circle continues, until we begin to see that universal light shining through our thoughts and motives, adding beauty to even the most difficult and shadowy parts of our existence.

It takes both. Without the light that spiritual consciousness radiates, our lives become dark recesses of despair, but without the adversities and trials of this physical world to provide the counterpoint, spirit cannot experience the joys of victory and growing self-knowledge. Yet viewed together they form beautiful patterns that give rich meaning to the tapestry of life.

Next time you are outside, look up into the heavens, knowing that whatever patterns you see are visible only because of the light source beyond. Take a few extra moments to appreciate the intricacies that our senses allow us to experience. And then think of your life, and know that all aspects of it can be transformed daily through allowing an awareness of the universal light of consciousness. This light, which permeates all of creation, is so imbued with wholeness of being, fullness of consciousness, and joyfulness of existence (*Sat, Chit,* and *Ananda* are the Sanskrit terms) that its presence transforms the patterns of our lives.

The light is always there. We just have to change our focus so that we can be open to the larger perspective of spirit. May the awareness of this light create beautiful patterns of hope and meaning in our lives through the dark of winter ahead and throughout the coming year.

WHAT TO WEAR

WHAT SHOULD I wear today? The purple sweater itches, and the green shirt is wrinkled. Besides, neither fits my mood today. What is it that makes us spend so much time considering our appearance? Some of us shop around for just the right look. Others carefully avoid the issue by wearing a standard "uniform" without noticing how attached they may be to a certain look.

When she is traveling, my mother loves watching people at the airport. She doesn't even feel the necessity to take along a good book for whiling away those hours of unexpected delays. Thousands of "books" parade before her eyes in the form of multitudes of weary travelers. Each one has a certain bearing, distinctive clothing, and a story to be told.

Being the rugged individualists that most Theosophists are, many of us might protest that we don't focus on outer appearances and thus don't pay so much attention to our garb. We like to think we are different. Actually, our costume is a part of the personality we use to interface with the world. Be it sloppy or neat, hip or out-of-step, our look reflects our culture and personality. It is a part of this incarnational package.

If you think you are not attached to your mode of dressing, try wearing something totally out of character and see how you feel.

The resulting self-conscious awkwardness can give a clue to how attached we all are to our particular character—the part we play in this world. We have a sense of our skin and the type of outer look that reflects who we are.

The strange thing about this world of illusion is that we pay so much attention to the outer garments without taking adequate notice of our inner garb. Most folks would not like to go out to meet the world each day without brushing their teeth and combing their hair, besides the usual last minute mirror-check. Yet few ever think of looking in that interior mirror to see if some adjustments need to be made.

When Jesus said that it is not what one puts into the mouth that corrupts, but what comes out of the mouth, he was referring to the importance of kindness of speech being far greater than compliance with religious dietary rules. A direct corollary to that axiom is that whatever is projected from within ourselves is far more important than however we adorn the outer self.

If this is so, we need to spend far more time looking into that interior mirror of our soul, and making the necessary adjustments. It would be so nice if this were as easy as changing clothes, but of course it is not. Yet if we wish to contribute to world peace and the uplifting of humankind, then concentrated attention must be given to our inner garments. When we look in the mirror, do we see the attire of irritability, frustration, anger, and impatience?

These characteristics, which are present in every one of us in varying degrees, are a part of the garments of our inner selves. Do you remember the Peanuts character, Pigpen? He carried a cloud of dirt swirling around his head wherever he went, scattering particles of dirt along the way. This image describes the way that our thoughts and emotions cloud our vision and contaminate those who come into our sphere. Even beyond that, our thoughts and feelings contribute to a far larger collective atmosphere that can affect many people for good or for ill.

If we are wearing kindness, tolerance, and a cheerful attitude, then we bring those qualities to all around us. On the other hand, we can add to the violence, unrest, and suspicion that permeate so much of our world if that is our outer garment. We can decide how we want to impact the world.

Taking poetic license with the evil queen in the fairy tale of Snow White, "Mirror, Mirror on the wall, I do not like this at all." If this is our response to the image we see, then we must take responsibility for changing our inner clothes. We may not like to be answerable for our attitudes, nor want to work to change them. Yet the fact of being responsible for and impacted by our thoughts and feelings is one of the unique traits of being human. Learning to take a mental bath is one of our essential tasks, but like Pigpen, we don't want to hop into the tub. Maybe if we would just try a little bit, we would find that it isn't so bad—maybe it is even pleasant.

Granted, our personalities are a product of long-time habitual attitudes; yet they are also plastic and subject to reprogramming one little bit at a time. If we notice our thoughts and feelings, they actually begin to transform before our very eyes. One could say that the light of clear consciousness is like a huge bar of soap, just waiting to scrub away the shadow. Not only that, but focused thought in the right direction can begin to reform our very natures.

We might consider a morning meditation as a standard part of the day just like brushing our teeth and combing our hair. Having a moment of quiet peacefulness, commitment to service, and the sending of kind thoughts to others every day is like bathing the personality in the purest cleanser. Although we may be encased in lots of crusty layers, and it may take weeks, months or years, gradually the true light of our being will shine through and we will be arrayed in all our natural splendor.

So tomorrow and the next day and the next, when you are deciding what to wear, think also about your inner self, how you would like it to be clothed, and what you would like for it to impart to the world. Then think about someone you love, feel peace in your heart, and start the day with a sense of gratitude for all the blessings around you. When you look in the mirror again, you will see that you have indeed put on your "Sunday best." You are ready for whatever the day may bring.

IT'S ABOUT TIME

THE SURREALIST ARTIST Salvador Dali, is perhaps best known for his paintings of melting clocks in a parched desert landscape. These haunting pictures reveal in symbolic language the arid nature of our own lives in modern society, controlled by the pressures of crowded schedules and impending deadlines. Close to the point of meltdown, it is difficult to find the space to be about the most important work of our lives—soul cultivation.

Many modern conveniences, which are supposed to save us time and theoretically create leisure time (an illusive dream for most of us), actually compound the intensity of our time constraints. The telephone makes it possible to keep in touch with an ever-increasing range of friends and family. Computers and faxes provide the opportunity to conduct almost instant—time business with people around the world. A written transmission is no sooner completed than the response has bounced back. Copy machines and emails duplicate more copies of documents for the expanding involvement of agencies, departments, personnel, and bureaucratic files. As rapid, long-distance travel shrinks the world, we have more places to go and less time to do so. This wealth of information and contacts would have been unthinkable a few generations ago!

In the face of these "luxuries" the challenge to maintain balance and contact with an inner atmosphere of quietude looms large. Is it possible to rush around, communicate effectively, and meet dozens of deadlines while still keeping in mind the sense of the inner self?

Perhaps those melting clocks are representative of the wasteland of our souls when we waste time—or spin out of control with misdirected energies. There are legitimately important tasks and they often fall on the busiest people, but it is because those busy people have learned to work with a balanced attitude. Although each one of us has our own limits, calm focused actions yield far greater results than jittery rushing motions. It is those nervous reactions to life that rob us of quality time. The more rushed we feel, the more exhausted and less effective we become.

In an odd self-defeating phenomenon, we become like tired little children who are avoiding going to bed. We get even busier doing irrelevant things, and crankier if we get any interruptions. This in fact becomes a way of life for us. Technology has so sped up this sensory impact that we don't know how to be quiet, and in fact we don't want to be. I know that when I have a big task ahead, it is easy to dissipate my energies on trivialities rather than focus on the one big item. We all have a tendency to fill our time with rushing to and fro so that we don't have to settle these over-active minds into a steady pattern.

A corollary to the high-speed information flow is an increased level of responsibilities for many of us. For each task that is accomplished, two more pop up, like the proverbial many-headed hydra. We don't know which task to attack next, knowing that more are always ready to materialize. So it is possible to feel paralyzed by the daunting mountain of tasks looming in the foreground.

Yet time is not the fixed commodity that it appears to be on the surface. Sometimes time hangs heavy, such as the span of time for young children from Thanksgiving to the Christmas holidays. In their world of heightened anticipation, time seems to go on forever. Alternatively consider the duration of a delightful vacation or intriguing task. In these cases the Latin adage "Tempus fugit" (time flies) applies. And whether happy or sad, consider the speed of time as we pass our mid-life point. Warp speed comes to mind. Time is flexible according to our mode of attention.

There is a place where clock-time does not exist. It is in the spaces of our inner being. These spaces can be experienced only in stillness. Relaxed focus is a way in which we can begin the stilling process. When the mind can focus on one particular task, shutting out all the others clamoring for attention, a calm descends. There is no longer a forest of confusion, but one tree that needs loving care. With attention, every detail of the task falls into place within a kind of timeless peacefulness. And interestingly enough, the other tasks that made up the undergrowth of the forest of confusion, begin coming into view one by one in clarity and simplicity. Full attention to the one thing attracts the energies of the inner self.

Focus or concentration is in fact a beginning stage of meditation. The mind, which is continually jumping around from one thing to another and generally drawn to the emotionally charged subjects around which it can forever chase its tail, can be trained to look at just one subject. Focus on the breath or a word works for some people, but for some it takes an object of adoration to keep the attention. In any instance the mind continually has to be reminded to stay on the one task; yet after a while it will begin to be more obedient.

Gradually the mind will have momentary clarity and peacefulness. The inner eye can look with greater objectivity at life, seeing what is real and what is not; important or not; possible or not. Then we can begin to manage time for personal well-being and to fulfill the calling of our higher nature (a kind of personal direction, known in the East as *dharma*). Then maybe we will be able to seize the moment and act with clear intention. When this happens, it will not be we who act, but the out-flowing nature of our higher selves. We will be operating "in the flow," in keeping with the Tao of Chinese philosophy.

In this way, if we begin to direct our focus and discipline our scattered minds, we can move out of the arid deserts of distorted time depicted in Dali's works into the green valleys of moments well spent. This transformation is possible if we spend some of our precious time in stillness, and carry that quiet focus out into the busy world. It is possible, however, only if we begin now.

It's about time!

I AM NOT WHAT I WAS

I LOVE EARLY morning walks. It is as if the day were so new that the first passersby cut through the expectant air, leaving swirls of possibility in their wake, like the bow of a ship disturbing the glassy surface of smooth water. Repeated walks seem to create a pattern in the air that strengthens with each repetition—like the visions reported by psychics of monks repeating their daily processionals hundreds of years after they have passed from the sight of human eyes.

This is especially true in one particular out-of-the-way place that I visit only occasionally. The passing years have hardly made a mark on the paths in the park or the cracked sidewalk by the schoolhouse. The same rail fence guards the pasture even though the old white mare no longer runs out to see if I might have an apple or two. I have passed these same spots since my youth. Sometimes that deja vu feeling becomes most intense. I feel almost as if I have entered a time machine and am walking in my previous presence—the shadows of times gone by.

There is a set of science fiction novels (Anne McCaffrey's *Dragonquest* series) in which the characters are able to ride dragons through time, arriving in a period earlier by centuries, or by days or hours. But their danger lies in getting too close to an encounter with themselves and, in the contradictions of time, becoming totally debilitated. Fortunately for me, my analogous experience is not real enough to do me in, but it is real enough to teach me an object lesson. No matter how close one comes to a repeat of time and place, there is never an exact repeat of the same conditions—most especially the condition of oneself.

The flow of consciousness continues and modifies with each new experience. Just as one can never put one's foot into the same stream of water a second time, so one cannot reenter the exact same space in consciousness. Change is a universal law, as postulated in Madame Blavatsky's second fundamental proposition concerning the makeup of our cosmos:

> This second assertion . . . is the absolute universality of that law of periodicity, of flux, reflux, ebb and flow, which physical science has observed and recorded in all departments of nature. An alternation such as that of Day and Night, Life and Death, Sleeping and Waking, is a fact so common, so perfectly universal and without exception, that it is easy to comprehend that in it we see one of the absolutely fundamental laws of the universe.

This translates to a universe that is in constant flux. Motion and constant change are fundamental characteristics of the entire manifested universe. This is certainly clear within our own stream of consciousness. Neither you nor I are the same from moment to moment. There are so many intervening moments of discovery, learning, pain, and joy. Whether one day has gone by or two months or thirty years, much has transpired to add to our storehouse of experiences that will translate into growth sooner or later. Sometimes we may have to repeat the same mistakes many times, but at some point the light will break through and we will at last say, "Ahaa!" We will finally get it and not need to repeat that particular lesson again.

If you have not seen the movie *Groundhog Day*, you have missed a good example of this very principle. Every time the protagonist awakens in the morning, it is the same Groundhog Day. Each day he repeats the same experiences, except that they change slightly because he is able to change his responses. It takes many times before he finally grows to the point that the outcome becomes what he would like it to be. He finally gets it.

The same sort of lesson can be derived from the cycle of a tree. Each spring when the tree issues its new growth, the leaves are not exactly the same as the year before but are reflective of the experiences the tree has garnered. If there are scars on the tree, or drought or insect damage, the new leafing pattern mirrors them. If a new branch has stretched forth into a spot of available sunshine, that too will be reflected. And so each year the tree, which of necessity remains in the same geographical spot, is ever new and ever formed by the previous seasons.

In every moment of our lives we can work to heal the wounds and grow new branches into the sun so that when we cycle through a situation again, we can be pleased with our progress. Whenever we return to similar circumstances, we will find ourselves the same in some ways, different in others.

If we pay attention to our lives, we can sense in the previous self a foreshadowing of the present version. In that moment we will realize that it took all of the former events to bring us to this particular place. We can begin to see the patterns and the meaning of it all. Why a particular occurrence happened still may not be totally clear, but we can honor the past as the vehicle that has brought us to this particular moment with all of its potentialities.

If we have worked well within our circumstances, then we can be pleased with the self that has grown beyond the one that passed this way before. In the process the past can finally fall into place, resolved as a part of the overall pattern of our journey.

This kind of alchemy can occur only if we live each moment the very best way we can. We must take each present moment to challenge ourselves to grow beyond our old way of interacting in the world so that when we pass this way again we will be able to see real progress. Then we will be able to say, "I may not be what I ought to be, but I surely am better than what I was."

FEED THEM AND THEY WILL COME

WHEN WE FIRST moved from the South to northeastern Pennsylvania, our kitchen window overlooked a backyard that was sparsely planted with a few large rocks and some struggling patches of grass. That first summer, we wondered if songbirds lived this far north, or much else for that matter. Except for the ever-present chipmunks, wildlife seemed scarce for a yard that backed up to a strip of woods.

Being nature lovers, we couldn't resist trying to transform our rough little patch of potential into something closer to paradise. Soon we had a variety of shrubs and flowers, a circulating fountain, and a number of bird feeders.

The yard bloomed and so did the wildlife. A pair of mourning doves moved in, followed by downy woodpeckers, finches, deer, and wild turkeys. We did discover the deer to be a questionable blessing (as anyone who has tried to grow any outdoor plants can attest), but overall we were pleased to see the parade of interesting "critters" through our little patch of paradise.

Children bloom in the same way when their inner natures are fed. The critical nutrients of love and feelings of value and self-worth need to be available in plentiful supply. Continual administrations of caring patience and interested attention create an environment that draws out the best qualities in the growing personhood of each little individual. Qualities of self-assurance, assertiveness, openness, and daring begin to gather within the developing ego.

Just as we saw the arrival of deer in our lush garden of delicacies, parents begin to see hints of a less pleasing picture as they enjoy the fruits of cultivating these qualities in their children. "No, I want to do it myself!" is the clarion call when parents are trying to rush the little darlings into readiness for a timely departure. And that's just the beginning. Then there are arguments over what to eat, what to touch, and when to go to bed, which in turn grow into discussions about homework, what to wear, and how late to stay out. This independence, such a desirable trait in an adult, is a most trying characteristic for parents to endure as it unfolds slowly over the years. (Yet when those years are behind us, it seems they were all too brief and we would bring them back if we could.)

However, sometimes our efforts bring unanticipated consequences. To return to the story of our backyard paradise, I can tell you that those woods harbored more than the aforementioned harmless creatures. They also harbored large bears. One morning we went out to find the one-inch steel rods that had held up our bird feeders twisted into grotesque shapes and the feeders strewn on the ground. And there at the back of the yard with a large rotund belly lay a black bear finishing off the last of the birdseed.

Being aware of the dangers of such a visitor, I called the local wildlife authorities and was told, "Lady, if you feed them, they will come." The only remedy offered was to stop putting out bird feeders. I was amazed that bears would be attracted to birdseed, but I have since learned that this is quite a common problem. Bears can smell fresh birdseed from miles away!

The growth of our own inner nature works in a similar way. First the newly developing ego needs to cultivate a sense of identity and strength, similar to humanity's development over eons. During those times the garden of self has to be nourished and encouraged to draw all things to it. But in maturity the focus must be changed. What were once necessary parts of our development can later become hindrances. Sometimes it takes an event like a visit from a bear to make us realize that it is time to change. Once we have gained strength of ego through careful care and feeding, a time comes when we must begin taking responsibility for the kinds of creatures that are coming to inhabit our minds.

As Madame Blavatsky so eloquently states in the Fragment III of *The Voice of the Silence*:

> Now, for the fourth prepare, the Portal of temptations which do ensnare the *inner* man. If thou would'st not be slain by them, then must thou harmless make thy own creations, the children of thy thoughts, unseen, impalpable, that swarm round humankind, the progeny and heirs to man and his terrestrial spoils.

Our thoughts are the children of our own making and they swarm around us, influencing all that we do for good or ill. Thoughts of harm to others, anger, selfishness, violence, degradation, pettiness, jealousy, and irritation (to name just a few) cling to us, creating a dense atmosphere and tripping us up at every turn. They were not the intended fruits when we first began our garden, but they were a part of our nature all along and finally materialized when they gained sufficient strength.

Within our inner sanctuary, we can scatter selected seeds. We can cultivate thoughts that are outwardly turned in an attitude of helpfulness and concern for others, or we can continue putting out the birdseed of selfishness and wonder why the bears keep coming to our doorstep. Every day, every moment, with every activity, we are deciding what aspects of ourselves we want to encourage. We can choose which kinds of thoughts we want to inhabit our world.

What are you attracting to your inner garden? Feed them and they will come.

DUST MATTERS

ONE OF THE inexorable matters of life is dust. It creeps in under windows and doors. It manufactures itself in the air. It is basically invisible until it has already produced a fine covering over everything around. As soon as it has been removed, dust resumes its march of conquest, defying any efforts to have everything "just so" even for a moment.

My mother who, at 91 years of age, has earned the family nickname of the "Eveready Bunny," has been an energetic householder all her life. Busy with an array of creative and service activities, she always viewed dust as a major nemesis. Although it is one of the lighter of housekeeping chores, it is one of the most odious to her and many other housekeepers.

During my growing-up years, Mother was fortunate enough to be able to hire someone to take care of the dusting, so I grew up unaware that dust actually collects on exposed surfaces. I assumed that it only accumulated in hidden corners and behind the books on my shelves. What a shock it was to this inveterate neat nick to discover, in my early married years, that relentless blanket gently smothering everything.

Every one of us encounters this same plight, within and without. Just as physical dust collects on our belongings, psychic dust blocks our access to the realm of spiritual clarity. Life experiences are the important ingredient in our human existence, providing the lessons we are here to learn. These experiences, necessary as they are, catch us in a karmic web of spiritual blindness. Things happen. We react in ways that we think will make our lives more to our liking. We become ensnared in our own little worlds. In other words, we have followed the natural path toward maturity by first becoming self-centered individuals.

Like the particles of dust swirling in the air which make the sunbeam visible, these experiences bring into focus our dharma, our purpose, the calling of our soul's pilgrim journey. The human predicament is to become fully invested in matter (life on this physical plane) and then to begin to clear away the emotional debris in order to wend our way home again.

Our humanity must reach the level of development at which we can learn how to dust! Inner dust is the accumulation of all the particles of experience that color our personality—the desires and avoidances. These are often referred to as attachments or patterns of desire, and are the emotional levers whereby karma works its power on us. In Hindu philosophy they are called the *skandas*, or the bundles of characteristics and predispositions that we carry with us from lifetime to lifetime.

The *skandas* are the third element in the nature or nurture argument concerning why people develop as they do. Anyone who doubts that a child arrives in this world with its own set of predispositions has only to experience the parenting of two children. Two children from the same gene pool and living in the same environment will be affected quite differently by the same event. One may remember a ride on an elephant as a major event, while the other barely takes notice, and so on. Even identical twins can reveal marked contrasts in personalities from the very start. One might imagine that the mirror of each child's soul has its own areas of stickiness, so that the dust collects more heavily in one area or another.

Wherever the dust is thickest, however, the fact remains that everyone has plenty of housecleaning to do. In *The Voice of the Silence*, H. P. Blavatsky speaks of the necessity of life experiences, or dust, in order to develop soul wisdom. But she says that the wisdom gleaned from life's lessons is only accomplished through regular dusting:

> *The seeds of Wisdom cannot sprout and grow in airless space. To live and reap experience the mind needs breadth and depth and points to draw it towards the Diamond Soul. Seek not those points in Maya's realm; but soar beyond illusions, search the eternal and the changeless SAT [the one eternal absolute], mistrusting fancy's false suggestions.*
>
> *For mind is like a mirror; it gathers dust while it reflects. It needs the gentle breezes of Soul-Wisdom to brush away the dust of our illusions. Seek O Beginner, to blend thy Mind and Soul.*
>
> *Shun ignorance, and likewise shun illusion. Avert thy face from world deceptions; mistrust thy senses, they are false. But within thy body—the shrine of thy sensations— seek in the Impersonal for the "eternal man"; and having sought him out, look inward: thou art Buddha.*

Although HPB uses the Buddhist idiom in this passage, in this instance the Buddha nature can equally be expressed as the Christ within, or the higher self. This nature is always within us just as a clean surface always resides beneath the dust, but it is beyond our awareness. In order to begin the cleansing process, we first have to be still, sitting quietly so that the gentle soul breezes can find their way into our hearts. Stillness is a beginning, but the sweeping requires the effort of objective self-observation and correction, and reliance on something higher or beyond the personal self—its foibles being the source of the dust. Separative and selfish attitudes cloud the mind-mirror and block our vision. In a little note at the end of letter 71 in the *Mahatma Letters to A.P. Sinnett,* Mahatma KH defines an enlightened being as one from whom:

> No curtain hides the spheres Elysian,
> Nor these poor shells of half transparent dust;
> For all that blinds the spirit's vision
> Is pride and hate and lust. . . .

And so dust we must. If we want to peer into our mirror mind, we have to clear the normal accumulation of personal attachments on a regular basis. Perhaps you can even use this metaphor when you have to clean dusty objects in your outer environment, to remind yourself of the need for removing self-serving matter from your inner world. This is the matter that really matters.

EVER NEW

HERACLITUS OF EPHESUS said that you can never step into the same river twice because new waters are always flowing around you. You might think it is the same river, but if you consider it for a moment, you will know that it is not exactly the same.

In fact, if water does not flow, it does not remain the same, but becomes stagnant. Change occurs in one way or the other. As Madam H. P. Blavatsky (HPB) said in *The Secret Doctrine* when describing the fundamental principles of the universe, motion and change are inevitable as a basic characteristic of manifestation:

> *This second assertion of the Secret Doctrine is the absolute universality of that law of periodicity, of flux and reflux, ebb and flow, which physical science has observed and recorded in all departments of nature. An alternation such as that of Day and Night, Life and Death, Sleeping and Waking, is a fact so common, so perfectly universal and without exception, that it is easy to comprehend that in it we see one of the absolutely fundamental laws of the universe. (p. 17)*

Although everything is in a state of change, some things are more obvious, such as the flow of water and the changes of the seasons. Others are more difficult to notice, such as the evolving changes in ourselves. The changes occur so gradually that we might not notice anything at all. And yet of all the changes in the universe, those wrought in our own consciousness are among the most profound. Humanity's purpose on this earth is to learn and grow through experience as a part of its unfoldment.

Understanding life's changes and working with them can make our lives a lot more pleasant and harmonious with the way things are. Our personal self wants to cling to the things we like and reject the things we don't like. Parents may want to stop the clock and cling to their children at certain cute ages, or to speed up the clock and avoid the difficult stage of the teenage years. Christmas never seems to come, but the end of a relationship or death of a loved one comes much too soon. Our attachment or avoidance of any situation makes the change appear to go very slowly or all too swiftly. Yet all these experiences lie within the inexorable flow of our consciousness.

To accept the changing flow of consciousness and to be able to deal at least somewhat dispassionately with the changes we all encounter are marks of spiritual maturity and bring healing to the sorrows of life. Our lack of flexibility in viewing ourselves, others, or situations blocks our clarity in seeing things as they really are. For instance, we may have grown greatly in our abilities to interface with people or to manage difficult situations, but if the little voice in our heads is repeating an old parental admonishment that we are not good enough, then we may still feel trapped at an earlier stage of development. Old habitual thinking therefore blocks our change and growth, just as a large rock may dam up a stream. Moreover, when we deal with others, if we cannot daily see them with fresh eyes, we might be doing them the same disservice by limiting their ability to grow and change in relationship with ourselves.

To realize that consciousness is like that river into which one can never step twice is to progress toward healing and growth. It is freeing to be able to look forward to the changes that occur and delight in the opportunities they bring. In Michael J. Roads' book, *Talking with Nature,* he relates how the flowing river taught him about the flow of consciousness. He recognized that consciousness is like the moving water of a river. Although the banks of a river or the body of a friend may look relatively unchanged for long periods of time, there is a constant motion and changing composition. And at every moment one must be able to overlook the relatively static outer form and relate to the newness of the inner life. Then our relationship will be ever new and vital, without the excess baggage of our history. This is a part of what Krishnamurti and other great teachers have meant when referring to "living in the present moment."

If we can tune in to this fresh perspective, we will be better able to tune in to the messages of meaning hidden in the world around us and be flexible enough to flow with the river of consciousness as it unfolds in ourselves and others. We will be able to allow ourselves and others to develop as needed, being ever new creations. Greet the possibilities that flow into each new day with thanksgiving.

FOR OTHERS

AS MY FRIEND explained the complicated ins and outs of his current minor difficulties, I lightly said, "I believe I had better start praying for you." Immediately my friend became agitated and insisted on not being the recipient of any prayers. To my incredulous questions he replied that in his experience, whenever people prayed for him, the intention was to direct or control him in some way—to impose their will on him.

After my first moments of shock, I realized the truth of this in many instances—especially in the context of praying so that someone "will see the light." The "light" is always defined as seeing the prescribed truths according to the one doing the praying.

H. P. Blavatsky writes in *The Key to Theosophy* that this is not prayer at all, but a kind of black magic:

> But woe unto those Occultists and Theosophists, who, instead of crushing out the desires of the lower personal *ego* or physical man, and saying, addressing their *Higher* Spiritual EGO immersed in Atma-Buddhic light, "Thy will be done, not mine," etc., send up waves of will-power for selfish or unholy purposes! For this is black magic, abomination, and spiritual sorcery. (67–69)

In other words, we cannot call on that universal power unless we first search our own hearts and fill them with a humble spirit, recognizing that we have no idea how to define the greater good even for ourselves, much less another. With this attitude we can align with highest spirit and truly pray a prayer of power.

Like the center of a walnut, there is within each person a strength of purpose which will unfold when the conditions are right. The outer husk may be tough and prickly and the center surrounded by bitter sheaths, but deep within is a soft, sweet core with the power to produce a mighty tree.

When we truly pray unselfishly for the good of another person, we support this center and call forth its power. We are not accomplishing something because of our own will, but when we tune in to the will of the infinite deific presence accessible in the still, secret chambers of our hearts, we can indeed move mountains. Continuing her discourse in *The Key to Theosophy*, HPB speaks of this God-Power within in the following way:

> Please say "God" and not *a* God. In our sense, the inner man is the only God we can have cognizance of. And how can this be otherwise? Grant us our postulate that God is a universally diffused, infinite principle, and how can man alone escape from being soaked through *by*, and *in*, the Deity? We call our "Father in heaven" that deific essence of which we are cognizant within us, in our heart and spiritual consciousness, and which has nothing to do with the anthropomorphic conception we may form of it in our physical brain or its fancy: "Know ye not that ye are the temple of God, and that the spirit of (the absolute) God dwelleth in you?"

In other words, this God essence is so all-pervading that it cannot be escaped. It is always present in ourselves and others but hiding under the crust of our day-to-day anxieties. Yet it is there, waiting in silence to be summoned forth. It is a transformational power that we can trust to be a steady force in our lives.

When I was visiting our daughter in Germany some years ago, I was struck by a political poster for the Green party. It depicted a patch of cracked asphalt with a triumphant blade of spring-green grass pushing its way through into the sunlight. The slogan proclaimed "Gruen bricht durch," or "Green breaks through." This powerful image has always stuck with me as a metaphor for the spiritual power trapped beneath the surface of our minds, waiting for the moment to break forth. It is a mystery rather than something to be understood intellectually. Committed intensity and pure intention, aligned with the universal good, bring the waters of unfoldment into the cracks of our consciousness, allowing the spiritual power to blossom forth against all odds. HPB refers to this as a transformational, alchemical process:

> Nor, as just remarked, that a prayer is a petition. It is a mystery rather; an occult process by which finite and conditioned thoughts and desires, unable to be assimilated by the absolute spirit which is unconditioned, are translated into spiritual wills and the will; such process being called "spiritual transmutation." The intensity of our ardent aspirations changes prayer into the "philosopher's stone," or that which transmutes lead into pure gold. The only homogeneous essence, our "will-prayer" becomes the active or creative force, producing effects according to our desire.

One of the greatest gifts given to us struggling human beings is the gift of being able to access this philosopher's stone for the good of all. Even if we don't say the right words, or know the most helpful hopes for the person for whom we are praying, we send a caring vibration through the universe that is carried on the wings of intentionality to help. The power of energy and support gently envelops the targeted recipient with the strength to reassert the natural impulse to wholeness and order.

So don't hesitate to participate. Tune in to an open, caring concern for your friends, neighbors, enemies, and strangers all over the world, and nourish those little blades of hope springing up and penetrating the darkness. Just as my friend finally concluded that he did indeed want to be included in my prayers, no one will want to hide from this kind of prayer. Its strength has the power to break the ravening darkness of the struggles of life and convert it to the greening pastures of hope.

SAND CASTLES

CHILDREN AND ADULTS can while away many hours building sand castles as they enjoy the lapping waves and warm sands on the seashore. A small child might begin awkwardly by filling up a bucket, packing the sand tightly, and then inverting it to create a magical flat-topped volcano standing prominently above the surrounding sand.

Over time, the child begins to imagine more complex creations: mountains, castles, roads, and tunnels. Sometimes interesting shells, toy cars, and action figures are added to enhance the growing fortress.

But eventually a stray animal or person comes running through, knocking the masterpiece helter-skelter, or the incoming tide over-reaches the water's former bounds and begins to dissolve it. At first the child may be disturbed that anything might tamper with such a work of art but soon must come to terms with its impermanence. As part of the learning process, and perhaps as an expression of frustration with a fickle universe, the child might begin tearing down the sand creations even before they are finished.

Children grow through the frustration, through the creativity, and through the rebuilding process. Gradually they become better sand castle builders. It doesn't matter if a wave washes everything away; it can always be rebuilt. Over time the growing person incorporates the skills until the sand castle always exists within potentiality—just waiting for the right sunny day at the beach.

In our daily lives, we are constantly encountering situations in which we must learn a new skill. As the skill develops, we create something—a house decorated, a picture painted, a paper written, or computer software designed. Each thing we do, although it may begin falteringly, becomes a matter of pride and attachment as we delve into the creative process. After investing so much in its formation, we slip easily into feelings of ownership and attachment to its permanence. As the Buddha said, clinging to the permanence of anything in this impermanent world causes a great deal of pain.

My work as a supervising systems analyst in state government with mainframe computer systems particularly brought this to my attention. Sometimes we would spend weeks or even months on a particular project, and just when it was really coming together, the entire definition of what we were trying to accomplish would change in the twinkling of an eye. This could happen for many reasons—changes in funding, in politics—but the fact was that a huge wave had washed over our machinations and we felt crushed. There were many things we could still be thankful for, of course— we still had our health, our paychecks, our families—but at the moment those didn't count. The team members were caught up in attachment to our investment in time, energy, and creativity. At such times it was helpful to take a step back and look at the bigger picture. I realized that it was much like a sand castle at the beach. Everything will change, and the tighter we hold on, the faster it will crumble.

But something can always be gained in the process that can never be taken away: our own inner resources and strengths. We develop the ability to build better sand castles. Whenever we apply ourselves fully to a task, no matter how the end product may turn out, we will have gained powers of concentration and greater skills.

If we apply ourselves to kindness and service, that too becomes a part of our inner tool chest. This is what Jesus meant when he said, "store up treasure in heaven, where neither moth nor rust will destroy nor thieves break in and steal." The great treasures that we are storing are tendencies and qualities of being—built by the ordinary days of our lives well-lived.

Hindu philosophy calls these bundles of characteristics *skandas*, those tendencies that are carried over from lifetime to lifetime, and very much a part of the mechanism through which karmic predicaments are met. The skandas become treasures as they are gradually transformed through our efforts in conscientious living.

The waves of time are not able to destroy the beauty of skill in action, single-minded commitment to the betterment of humanity, and a loving heart. These will continue as lasting treasures—the sand castles stored within us.

ONE FOR THE ROAD

SOME TIME AGO during a speaking tour I had to take a limo from Los Angeles to Long Beach, California. Being unfamiliar with the territory, I could give only the street address of my destination and leave the rest up to the driver, who exhibited all of the most exciting traits of his high-spirited, risk-taking fellow taxi drivers in other major cities around the world. Since he did not know the targeted destination, he decided to look up the street index and search his map while he was careening in and out of the heavy traffic on the infamous southern California freeways. For all the attention he seemed to be paying to the road in front of him, he might as well have pasted the index and map over the windshield of the car. After what seemed an eternity and a few prayers in the back seat, we finally did arrive safely—shaken, but none the worse for the wear.

Reflecting on the experience later, I realized that many of us live life in just this way. There are many resources that can be used as roadmaps for life. Some may use religious texts, some schools of psychology, or others the teachings of a guru. All may sound intriguing or erudite, or even have the ring of truth, and so we are drawn to studying and discussing them endlessly. For many Theosophists this kind of mental exploration can be exhilarating and captivating. We feel that we are just one tiny step away from knowing the secrets of life.

Scientific discoveries that confirm some of our pet theories excite us and draw us further into our theoretical explorations. Without a doubt I must affirm, as H. P. Blavatsky so often did, that science is a powerful ally in our earnest search for truth. At the empirical gross physical level, it can confirm many ideas about our universe. From those ideas we can draw implications for the meaning and purpose of life, but those ideas have no substance unless they are acted upon.

Lacking a map in unfamiliar territory we might wander aimlessly through wrong turns and dead-ends. We have a hard time finding pleasure in the trip because of our pent-up anxiety. Gradually we develop a map in our mind that serves as our guide and we reach a certain level of comfort in following the known routes. At this point, not wanting to risk a return to our former state of confusion, we may be resistant to change. We may even refuse to consider others' advice or new maps.

Maps are important and necessary. When we finally look at a detailed map it can be a real eye-opener. We may have been going the long way around, or taking the stoplight-ridden route when there was a far simpler way to go. And there may be a lovely park to traverse rather than a busy street. Maps are wonderful tools. They can give us an overview of an area as well as pinpoint details. But they are not the territory itself.

In our spiritual lives, an encounter with a source of spiritual guidebooks such as our Theosophical literature can be an exciting discovery. All of a sudden we can gain a higher view and clearer idea of detours and pitfalls. Many of us have experienced that heightened intensity of study in the early years of our Theosophical or metaphysical pursuits. A new world of understanding arises. The territory of life is far different from what we had first thought; the scheme grander and more meaningful. We discover a holistic approach that integrates all aspects of religion, philosophy, science, and the arts.

In the excitement we can become so caught up in the map that we forget it is not the territory. We become like the driver who has the map pasted across the windshield, and forget to watch the traffic, landmarks, and road signs. Self-absorption in studies becomes counterproductive, blocking the very clarity, understanding, and direction we are seeking.

As H. P. Blavatsky admonishes all Theosophists in *The Key to Theosophy*:

> No working member should set too great value on his personal progress or proficiency in Theosophic studies; but must be prepared rather to do as much altruistic work as lies in his power. He should not leave the whole of the heavy burden and responsibility of the Theosophical movement on the shoulders of the few devoted workers. Each member ought to feel it his duty to take what share he can in the common work, and help it by every means in his power.

Periodically we have to remove our noses from our books and our minds from endless titillating theories in order to put our knowledge into practice, or we will never unfold our spiritual natures. Our studies provide the map, but they have to be balanced by service and meditation. Meditation is the actual vehicle that will carry us into the unfoldment of our spiritual potential, and service is the essential fuel. Both are supported by the maps found in our studies, and both require actual commitment.

Remember fellow pilgrim, when you are studying those books,

that they may well be helpful maps for understanding and navigating the territory, but the trip involves engagement on the path. If our study is to be useful, every new understanding should help us discern the real from the unreal, the more important from the less important, and make us better prepared to travel. Each small step that we take on this journey is a giant leap for humankind. So let us take that first step—and the next—and the next—that begin and continue the journey of the rest of our lives.

Bon Voyage!

WHAT IS TRUTH?

MANY TRUTHS, accepted through the ages, are not as strong and formidable as they may seem. From time to time an intellectual storm of explorers—philosophers or scientists—can shake our certainty and expose the faulty core of our suppositions.

The famous Albert Einstein, still in his mid-twenties, broke beyond the boundaries of thought in his time. He had not been a good student because he would not learn by rote, but had to explore the questions in depth for himself. Of course he had a penetrating intellect, but it would have done him little good without the willingness to explore outside the accepted paradigms. In 1905 he published four papers—two explaining how to measure the size and speed of molecules in a liquid, another how light is composed of photons (the foundation of quantum physics), and finally the Nobel Prize—winning theory of the relativity of time and space. Only a few months later he published a paper on the interchangeability of matter and energy with his famous equation of $E=mc^2$.

Science is still reeling from his discoveries, uncovering new implications every year. Einstein's theories are an extreme example, but they illustrate how far-reaching a few new ideas can be when they become a part of basc knowledge for subsequent truth seekers to build upon.

Whether in the outer world of scientific discovery or in the explorations of our own consciousness, an open mind is the essential vehicle that takes us on our journey. Our finite minds can relate only to very small corners of the truth, and because of that our observations can be distorted and our conclusions faulty. Consider, for example, the story of the blind men studying an elephant: one examining the trunk proclaims the animal to be like a giant snake; another posted at its leg declares it to be like a tree; and yet another at its side vows that any intelligent person can tell that it is not an animal at all but a giant wall. The picture can be expanded to whole nations or cultures standing in the place of each of the blind men. Partial truths can be very entrenched and very misleading.

In his earliest writing (*At the Feet of the Master*) J. Krishnamurti, who was known for his efforts to free our minds from preconceptions and attachments, spoke of the need to distinguish truth:

> in thought first; and that is not easy, for there are in the world many untrue thoughts, many foolish superstitions, and no one who is enslaved by them can make progress. Therefore you must not hold a thought just because many other people hold it, nor because it has been believed for centuries, nor because it is written in some book which men think sacred; you must think of the matter for yourself, and judge for yourself whether it is reasonable. Remember that though a thousand men agree upon a subject, if they know nothing about that subject their opinion is of no value. He who would walk upon the Path must learn to think for himself, for superstition is one of the greatest evils in the world, one of the fetters from which you must utterly free yourself.

"There is no religion higher than truth," the inspiring motto of the Theosophical Society, means that at all times, no matter how wonderfully coherent our theories are, the flexibility to accommodate new understandings is a necessary component of spiritual growth. When new knowledge or insight sweeps through like a summer storm, we can use it to nourish our spirit as we journey into new areas of maturity. If we deny a truth's presence, we create a blockage that will obstruct the source of our nourishment. It is this kind of rigidity that causes people to become frightened believers, rejecting change and debasing science and religion into a kind of superstition. As the saying goes, "They do not want to be confused by the facts because their minds are already made up." People can be deeply wounded by the winds of encroaching knowledge contrary to their belief structures.

This was a major theme throughout the writings of Madame Blavatsky. She wanted to debunk the gross materialism of scientists and the narrow superstitions of the religious leaders of her day. Her desire that humanity might be freed from these fetters echoed the purposes of the teachers who stood behind her. In her dogged dedication to truth she urged all to cultivate an open mind and an eager intellect in order to move toward spiritual maturity.

Later in his life Einstein rejected an early pet theory—the idea that in order for the stars to stay in place, moving relatively so slowly through space, there must be some kind of antigravity. When Hubble's discovery that the universe is expanding at great speeds eliminated the need for this theoretical force to keep stars from collapsing into each other, Einstein decided that his antigravity theory no longer fit. He was willing to let go of a cherished idea. Interestingly, however, years later the rejected idea of the repulsive effects of antigravity, now called dark energy, might be the cornerstone for understanding the force that is driving our ever-expanding and accelerating cosmos.

The fluctuation in the perceived verity of Einstein's theories reflects the path to truth for each of us. Open-mindedness is required for useful exploration and discrimination at every step. Sometimes a realization of a truth may have beneficial reverberations through the years, and these instances are to be gratefully nurtured. Sometimes as the data trickles in, we may realize that we were operating under faulty conceptions and we need to move beyond them. And sometimes in our growth we may reject a thing as untrue but later have to consider it as a truth on a new level. Even ideas we have discarded for good reason at one time may be discovered to be valid in a different context or at a deeper level.

Some of our religious background may fall into this category. Even though our early religious training may have been dogmatic and constrictive, the faith idiom underlying those teachings may yet have powerful mythic meaning that can speak to the depths of our psyche. In such a case open-mindedness includes being willing to modify judgment on discarded truths if that is found to be useful.

What ideas might we be clinging to that we need to open to fresh understanding? Are there any things we have discarded that we may need to reexamine? Can we look at our inner and outer worlds with new eyes so that the storms of life nourish us rather than break us? If we are willing to explore our worlds based on experience, study, and meditational insight, our life-roots will reach deeply into wisdom and truth. In this context truth seems to be a product of the search rather than any static reality. We might even loosely translate the Theosophical motto to be: "There is no better way to seek union with the divine than to be earnestly searching for it."

AS A CHILD

WITH THE RECENT arrival of our first grandchild, I am reminded not only of the beauty and significance of life but also of our dependence on each other for survival and well-being. One wonders how any mother and child ever survive without professional and family support. There have been and still are those situations in which this happens; the conditions are harsh and survival tenuous. Yet within community it can become a beautiful and nurturing experience.

Aspirants who first decide to set foot on the spiritual path are similar to a newborn. Like an infant they awaken to a strange world where they require much attention, for which they have no skills, and yet in which they have infinite potential.

One of the first requirements for the neophyte is some type of nurturing attention. There are very few in this world who, like the Buddha, can sit unaided under the Bodhi tree and find enlightenment or, like Jesus, can emerge unscathed from forty days of temptations in the wilderness, fully conscious that he and the creator/sustainer are one. Even in those instances various teachers who had contributed to their preparations.

Because these two supreme examples are far beyond the ken of most of us mere mortals, we are more like infants or at best growing children, playing at the edges of understanding life and its purposes. We all require the support of wise teachers through

63

the written and spoken word, the good examples of our fellows' achievements, and, most important, caring interaction with a community focused on the spiritual life.

We need to find a community of like-minded people, those who don't think we are crazy for not following the usual pattern of self-interested materialism. Fellow seekers can share in our search for understanding, provide a sounding board for our nascent ideas, and point us toward expanded horizons for exploration.

The awakened spirit within us is much like an ember in a camp-fire. If separated too far from the warmth of the blaze, our flame will flicker and lose its heat. Our consciousness responds to the spiritual heat of those around us and can lose its direction when constantly impacted by the materialistic and self-focused influences so rampant in the surrounding darkness.

Often termed the Sangha, a spiritual community does not have to provide physical proximity, although that is extremely useful. Some contact does have to occur, and of course face-to-face contact is always best, but in our mobile society with a limited proportion of spiritual seekers, that kind of contact may be sporadic at best. The Theosophical Society was founded to be a nucleus of the universal brotherhood of humanity. That means it was intended to be a center that could attract the glowing embers of souls to spark their own flames, cultivate the blaze in each other, and draw newcomers toward the heat.

In volume 14 of the *Collected Works of H. P. Blavatsky*, she affirms: "The first and fundamental principle of moral strength and power is association and solidarity of thought and purpose." She recognized that we must come together as a nucleus of humanity in order to survive and develop into our potential. Ours is not a simple task but a complex, difficult project.

As newborns, not only do we need the warmth of support, but

we have an interior mountain to climb. We arrive on the scene with limited awareness and capabilities, and through many struggles gradually unfold the abilities to see, to hear, to speak, and to act in accord with higher principles. Persistence and patience with ourselves and in interactions with others as these abilities develop are the bedrock for a strong footing in this climb.

There will be many a faltering step as we develop the skills to live in the new world we are trying to enter. We have to learn to function on every level in an entirely different way from the one we have known. These tasks are described in *Light on the Path*, one of our treasures of esoteric literature:

> Before the eyes can see, they must be incapable of tears. Before the ear can hear, it must have lost its sensitiveness. Before the voice can speak in the presence of the Masters it must have lost the power to wound. Before the soul can stand in the presence of the Masters its feet must be washed in the blood of the heart.

With our realized dependence and connections with others, and a clear commitment to the process of growing our capacities, we share a third similarity with the infant. Unlimited potential awaits us as our future splendor unfolds. We will one day be the wise ones who serve as guardians to humanity. As Madame Blavatsky put it, "For those who win onwards there is reward past all telling—the power to bless and save humanity . . ." (*Collected Writings*, vol. 13)

As they gaze at their children, parents wonder who these little people are. What will they be? What wonders will unfold as they develop? How will they add to the beauty of the world? Optimism pervades most reactions to these little ones because of the many possibilities abiding in latency. We recognize that there may be many a stumble and difficulty but that those are also a part of the growth process.

The development of our potential should spark determined perseverance in working on ourselves and investing effort in banding together with like-minded individuals who can serve as the core of hot coals that both warms and challenges us. We need community as much as any young creature struggling for survival.

If we keep the image of a developing child in mind as we try to grow, and as we interface with our compatriots in this effort, then we will be able to have greater understanding and see things from a larger perspective. Instead of the flawed human beings of the present, we will be able to see the beauty in latency. When we look in the mirror or into the window of our fellows' heart, we will perceive the potential of purity and wisdom. We will see wise ones in the making.

THE FIELD OF MEMORIES

MY MOTHER AND I have been going through old photo albums and letters from my dad written over seventy years ago. They bring back the memories of many happy moments. The letters in particular paint a word picture of the quite remarkable man my father was—sensitive and profoundly philosophical for a young person. These and other not-so-well-documented memories blend with the present to form the background of personal history that I carry with me. They are a part of the continuity that is my self.

For everyone this field of memories is a mixed backdrop of the good, the bad, the bittersweet, and the joyous. Some things we are most glad to have finished and relegated to the past; yet occasionally we worry them with our minds just as the tongue keeps seeking out the sore place. And those times that we wish would last forever all too quickly recede into the eddies of time.

These elements blend to weave a rich tapestry that gives definition and meaning to the "who-ness" of what we are. There may be things we would like to forget and things we would like to cling to—ever unchangingly. Neither changing the past nor clinging to a static, changeless present is possible. But the past is modifiable depending upon how we ride the karmic patterns as they flow through our lives.

Each day the only moment is now. This "now" even at this moment has already receded into the passing shades of time. This baffles the mind and so it grasps the present moment in such a way as to make us feel that "this is it." It acts somewhat like the distortions of a magnifying glass. Those events that are nearest its center focus are magnified to larger than life, but very quickly, as the glass drifts toward a new scene, the former experience becomes fuzzy. It does not usually hold our attention any longer, but if it does, the situation is seen in a warped manner. We are usually sure that we are clearly remembering the event exactly as it happened, but as any investigator of a crime scene will attest, the view of every witness is distorted by his or her particular perspective.

We humans have the power to determine what some of our memories will be. We establish birthday and anniversary observances so that we can mark our lives with celebrations and touchstones. Even the universal countdown to a new year, ringing out the old and welcoming the new, brings resolutions for change and hopes for the future. For our children and for ourselves we establish traditions that are intended to bring happiness to all.

Ah, but does it always happen this way? Sadly, it does not. The dish breaks; Uncle John gets mad; little Joe gets hurt. Things just don't turn out according to plan. As is said about the plans of mice and men, things oft go awry.

Yet we have an even greater power. We can choose what to focus on, what to pay attention to, what to magnify. A picnic overrun with ants may be held on a beautiful day in a lovely setting. When a bee sting no longer hurts, one can relish the blessings of normal, healthy skin. Even in the midst of stress or tragedy, we each have the power to lift our eyes to the wider view that encompasses many blessings.

Even when his charges were suffering and dying in the Vietnam

War, the Vietnamese Buddhist monk Thich Nhat Hanh was able to remain mindful of the simple blessings of life. His teachings and presence were, and continue to be, an inspiration to many. He has taught his followers to be mindful of the present moment, one breath at a time, and to smile. This may seem simple, but it is amazingly profound. The practitioner builds a field of gentle thoughts and memories even in the midst of strife.

With this power comes opportunity and responsibility. We can actually select what materials we will use in building our interior landscape. We can people our inner world with pleasant moments that translate into pleasant memories as they glide by our consciousness. Like the cloud of dust that hangs around the head of Pigpen, the character in the *Peanuts* comic strip, these thoughts—as Madam Blavatsky tells us in *The Voice of the Silence*—remain with us and swarm around our heads:

> If thou would'st not be slain by them, then must thou harmless make thy own creations, the children of thy thoughts, unseen, impalpable, that swarm round humankind, the progeny and heirs to man and his terrestrial spoils.

During any particular event we can pay attention to the problems that are occurring, or the help received from a friend, or, if nothing else, the joy of breath or health. When a hurt or an illness heals, we can savor the joys of a vibrant spirit or a vigorous body.

We can choose not only what to pay attention to in the moment, but also what to cultivate in our memory banks. Although it is true that our thoughts are wild and hard to tame, with steady focus we can direct them. We can notice our thoughts and work to corral them in a positive direction. If it is useful to review an old hurt, we can do so with the aim of healing and bringing closure—never to relish a vengeful or hurt attitude.

Humanity has been granted the unique power of creativity. Every moment of every day we are creating our field of memories. These will swarm around us for either good or ill. A most critical use of that power is to people our world with at least harmless "children" and hopefully with helpful ones. Daily we can build that field with warm and nourishing memories by directing our attention to the Good within every moment. In this way our thoughts are able to lighten our own lives and create an atmosphere that fosters blessings for all beings. May you cherish and use wisely this most marvelous power as you cultivate your field of memories in the coming year.

A NEW LIFE

IN THE MOVIE *Doctor Zhivago*, "Laura's Theme (Somewhere My Love)" gently encourages hopes of spring and new life as the scene shifts to fields of daffodils swaying in the breezes. After terrible disasters for most of the players in the story, this is a respite of hope and new beginnings. As with most of us however, the characters still carry baggage from their past that will catch up with them.

A part of the human condition is to have to face challenges and disappointments. Whether it is something that could not be averted, such as the natural disaster of Hurricane Katrina, or whether caused by human error, bad things happen to everyone. As the politicians say, "Mistakes were made." And usually it is a combination of our actions plus unforeseen events.

These difficulties fill our minds with angst and worry. We may have an equal share of serendipitous occasions but we tend to quickly forget about those. It is more difficult to let go of the unpleasant. It seems to be built into our nature that when we see a large piece of white paper with one tiny smudge, it is the smudge that catches and holds our attention.

I had an uncle who had worked all his life building up a combination dry cleaning and bakery business. A kind and honest man, he had lived and worked in the same small town all his life. During the process of trying to sell his businesses so that he could retire, he was swindled out of the entire enterprise with barely a nickel to show for all his work. Had he been able to let go of his resentment, he would have had a pleasant existence for the next 15 years of his life. With full ownership of his house and minimal expenses in the small town, he could have enjoyed his friends, family, and grandchildren. Instead he lived every day of his remaining 15 years with bitterness.

This is only one of many similar instances in which the ability to begin again with a clean slate would be beneficial. If one could let go of the old attachments, even while remaining in the same situation, there could be a fresh start with renewed possibilities.

When considering the idea of reincarnation, many question why we do not remember past lives. Many not only question, but actively seek former identities and relationships. The romanticism of being someone else—preferably of heroic stature—salves the strain of current problems. They may do well to appreciate the value of beginning with a clean slate, viewing their present life and situation with new eyes.

Babies bring with them the hopefulness of infinite potentiality. They arrive without baggage, open to a new world. There is no question that from the beginning they bring a particular personality with qualities of being and preferences. Ah, but how fortunate they are that they can take each new experience with an unfettered approach. Jesus was referring to this kind of attitude when he said, "You must become as a little child to enter the kingdom of heaven."

Reincarnation involves the big picture of new beginnings, but is something over which we have very little control. In the present, however, we can be born anew. This is not a birth of the body, but one of attitude and spirit. With each new day and in every moment of that day, we can open our eyes to things as they are in the moment—just as Krishnamurti and many other spiritual teachers have reminded us. Then we can have clarity and the space to make wise decisions.

This teaching was expressed by the Buddha when explaining his Noble Eightfold Path. As Madame Blavatsky said: "[The Buddha's] efforts were to release mankind from too strong an attachment to life, which is the chief cause of Selfishness—whence the creator of mutual pain and suffering." (CW VIII, 112)

"Attachment" carries many nuances of meaning, but in all it refers to clinging—usually to the past and always to the way we want things to be. The memories to which we cling imprison our greater nature by replaying the past. Possibly the reason our universe is designed so that we have limited lifetime lengths is to give us the necessary break from the past, and to grant us the gift of new beginnings.

This kind of renewal is possible, but as Krishna acknowledges in the *Baghavad Gita*, the mind is most difficult to tame. Yet with persistent effort, it can be accomplished. Daily we can practice the idea of experiencing life anew. Every morning that we arise, we can think of the spring daffodils dancing in the breezes of time, beckoning us to try again. We can determine that this is the beginning of a new life with infinite possibilities.

FOLLOW THE FLOW

WHEN A MAGNET is held near metal filings, the filings flow into different patterns, depending on the location, strength, and polarity of the magnet. Even after the obvious pattern has formed, there are usually a few stragglers that hop, skip, and jump into place at the last minute, as if they had been held back, or were asleep when the first tug came. But they cannot resist the constant pull of an almost magical invisible force, undetectable by our five senses.

Each of us is like a magnet in the way we repeatedly attract similar people and circumstances. Just as soon as one bad relationship ends, another takes its place. When we escape negative issues in employment one place, we find the same in another. You can often discover how well a new resident will like a town by their answer to the question, "How did you like where you just came from?" Wherever we go, we carry a kind of attraction for similar outcomes. Karma and habitual attitudes follow us like the cloud of dust seen over Pigpen, the Peanuts cartoon character who never takes a bath. Sometimes, it may seem that we have a sign over our head that says, "Hit me!" or "Sock it to me!" as on the old *Laugh In* show.

This principle goes both ways; positive people and circumstances are also drawn to us. However, we tend not to notice the serendipitous events, because we generally do not question the good times, only the bad. When things go well, we may enjoy ourselves so much that we don't feel the urge to analyze or philosophize. Yet, because life has its own flow and cyclical nature, it is wise to pay attention whatever the experience.

It is not necessarily that we draw all adversity directly to ourselves, or that we deserve every bad thing that happens—thereby indicating our unworthiness. Rather, it is a complex concatenation of causes and potentialities that flow together—like a dance, or those metal filings. In the subtle realms of connectivity, our higher self, perhaps in conjunction with the Lords of Karma, attracts to our personality those elements of experience which draw us toward our potentiality. Sometimes, it may be a shock that acts as a wake-up call to redirect our energies; sometimes, disappointments or pain deepen our connections with the inner realities; while at other times, serendipitous happenings catapult us into a whole new arena of growth and service.

> However it might manifest, the purposefulness of random events unfolds for the student of life. Madame Blavatsky spoke of this phenomenon by referencing a Roman legend. Once when Rome was threatened by attack, a lone goose cried out, perhaps in its sleep, and woke the entire flock. The cries of the disturbed birds alerted the sentries and thereby saved Rome.
>
> Has it never struck you, that if the nightmare of a dreaming goose, causing the whole slumbering flock to awake and cackle—could save Rome, that your cackle too, may also produce as unexpected results? ... But don't you know, that the building of a nest by a swallow, the tumbling of a dirt-grimed urchin down the back stair, or the chaff of your nursery maid with

the butcher's boy, may alter the face of nations, as
much as can the downfall of a Napoleon? Yea, verily
so; for the links within links and the concatenations
of this Nidanic* Universe are past our understanding. (*Collected Works*, vol. 12, 384–5)

None of this cause and relationship is static or linear. Every
attitude and action we take blends with all the potential circumstances emerging from everyone around us, and cureates a new set
of possibilities. As we learn and grow beyond the circumstances
of yesterday, the whole pattern can dissolve and shift, so that what
was once an insurmountable problem can dissolve like a mist in
the midday sun.

The fluidity of what seemed to be unshakably set circumstances
has often proven true in my own experience. My once-dreaded
boss who seemed to delight in setting me up for certain stumbles,
if not total failure, faded into the background as I gained my own
strength in dealing with her. As soon as I had fully conquered the
situation in myself, I was promoted away from what had seemed
like an interminable ordeal.

Another time it seemed that crumbling finances would bring
down my house of cards. But as I faced each issue and worked my
way through it, what had looked like a certain brick wall faded into a
pathway—a little rocky, but a pathway, none the less. By conquering
the difficulty within myself, the actual outer circumstances meta-
morphosed into something that could be handled.

I have become strongly convinced that all of life is a gigantic
synchronistic flow for the purpose of spiritual unfoldment, which
is somehow orchestrated by our higher selves, in harmony with

Nidanas, or the concatenation of causes and effects, in the Eastern philosophy.

76

the greater power beyond our ken. Whatever is drawn to us is not at all related to the wishes of our personality. In fact, it very often seems to be the opposite. But it is in line with creating the possibilities for us to become all that we can be.

By paying attention to this directivity in our lives, we can discover our true nature and calling. In this discovery lies the possibility that we can find joy in following the flow, instead of feeling torn and tossed. We can actively cooperate with the magnetic pull of the universe toward growth, evolution, and wholeness.

IN TUNE

THE SCREAMING SIREN pierced my quiet meditation. Although I should have been beyond the impact of the five senses, my ears caught the sound and insistently roused my responses. Sirens were designed with just that annoying characteristic in mind. They are intended to cut through our consciousness and to startle us into alertness. Moreover, because of their purposes, sirens are harbingers of disaster, crisis, or at the least, bad news, as in the case of a police car fast approaching.

Sound is vibration in the air waves that becomes intelligible to us because of the apparatus in our ear canals and the brain's ability to sort the vibratory messages received into meaningful information. This calls to mind the age old question, "If a tree falls in the forest where there is no one to hear, does it make any noise?" The vibration may be there, but is it only sound when it is translated into such by a receptor?

Whether or not the receptor is present to respond, the vibration is real and has its impact. If it were possible for a deaf opera singer to sound such a piercing note, whether anyone was present to hear it or not, that note could still shatter glass. The vibration is a physical fact, with a physical impact regardless of our presence or ability to perceive it.

Sound is defined as vibration within the range of hearing, but the range is quite variable, diminishing with age or trauma to the ears. We generally would not classify the high-pitched dog whistle as sound, except for the fact that we recognize the dog's response.

Some time ago I read that law enforcement was experimenting with the use of low-pitched inaudible sound as a way to help control riots. The idea was that this very low vibration could confuse people's mental processes and thus diffuse their angry intentions. I don't know about this, but I do know that after a long ride in a plane or car, for a brief while I feel more muddled than usual. Could this possibly be the impact of that steady deep vibration, rather than the fatigue factor?

Sound is a small but powerful range of vibration close to our physical existence. From sonic boom to heavy drumbeat, we cannot deny its power. But it is an accessible range of vibration that provides a metaphor for the whole arena of our manifested universe. All of creation consists of a complex multitude of vibrations. This is why several traditions refer to that first creative impetus as "the Word."

From Hindu tradition, the story of Indra's net expands this idea of the vast impact of any small sound or vibration on the whole. Indra, the king of the gods and the ruler of the heavens, has a palace above which is suspended an enormous net extending infinitely in all directions. This net consists of a myriad of interconnected junctions of a fine mesh, with each junction being responsive to all the others. The legend has each connecting point set with a jewel that reflects all the others in its many facets. Some have called these sensors bells that resonate with all other sounds; while others have compared them to mirrors reflecting the faces of all living beings. If these points of interconnection were defined in today's vernacular, they might be called holographic points. Whatever the image, the message is clear. What is done to one being impacts all beings.

The whole is a living system that thrills in response to even the smallest occurrence.

We are vibratory creatures. To each of us individually, our vibration may seem to be dense and of little impact, but that is a false message delivered to us by this illusory world. Not only are we constantly bombarded by the whole of our world culture, but we are also contributing to that culture minute by minute. We transmit the vibration of our being into this milieu, impacting ourselves most of all, but also creating a resonance that sounds around the world.

If we could but control the message we send forth, what a difference it would make. It is difficult, but we can monitor and modify the words and actions that we generate. Yet how much more difficult it is to tame the mind and emotions. And herein lies the key. The greatest transmission we emit is not an external one, but a transmission of the very nature of our being. How often have we heard that to find the path, we must become the path? Our actions, words, and thoughts are the building blocks of the resonating chamber of our nature. If we want to have peace, we have to be peace.

Consider any outburst you may have had against another, or any time you felt superior to another, knowing that you are absolutely right. These are the seeds of fanaticism and violence that contribute to our current international plight. Not one of us wants to contemplate the possibility that we are a part of this cycle of attack and retribution; yet the "enemy" is a reflection of us and we are compelled to begin to heal ourselves and rein in our thoughts.

This is the task that is set before us. Personal transformation is the pathway of Theosophy and all quests for Truth. With sustained effort we can regulate our attitudes and actions, and little by little we can change our keynote to one of compassion and concern for all. Then the vibration of our being will be able to permeate the atmosphere, not with the distress of a siren, but with the call to responsible living and the music of altruism.

> Hast thou attuned thy heart and mind to the great mind and heart of all mankind? For as the sacred River's roaring voice whereby all Nature-sounds are echoed back, so must the heart of him "who in the stream would enter," thrill in response to every sigh and thought of all that lives and breathes. (*Voice of the Silence*)

WATCH IT

AS SOON AS the first rays of daylight peep through the edges of our window shades, my cat perches on her viewing table at a particular window of interest. After about fifteen minutes, patience wearing thin, she begins a gentle tapping at the shade, softly at first, but quickly building to a level to compete with any rock band. We of course express our gratitude to her for eliminating any need for an alarm clock, and then drag blearily out of bed in order to accommodate her feline curiosity.

Thus begins the day of watchfulness over the squirrels and birds, which seem to deliberately cavort in that particular spot just to tease her. The intense vigil is punctuated by occasional breaks for food, affection, naps, and frolicking. At her post, however, there is no room for lapses into laziness. Whiskers and ears forward, marking every movement beyond the window, she is poised for that one moment when the glass might disappear, giving her full access to the ground below with all its tantalizing inhabitants.

Living in two worlds at the same time, our cat exemplifies the kind of attitude we might develop through a committed vigil of silence. Anyone familiar with cats knows that they do not in any way neglect their creature comforts. In the fashion of Garfield, they are known for their luxuriating habits. Yet, they become fully alert and ready to pounce at the slightest appearance of a target. They live every moment attuned to their daily needs but always seem to have an inner radar tuned to other possibilities.

We also live in two worlds at the same time, but we mostly live in a state of forgetfulness concerning the world of reality that waits in the inner silence. A world of strength, potentiality, and certainty does exist through the interior window of our being, but we forget to be attuned to it, to have that daily vigil of alert watching. The ordinary activities of our lives, minds, and emotions create a cacophony that drowns out other possibilities. Perhaps we need to consider exploring that inner alertness every morning in order to carry that kind of attunement all day long.

Far more important than the cavorting squirrels, that interior space contains the patterns and causes of the present situation as well as the source of wisdom as to how to work within and through it. Theosophy teaches, and many of us have begun to realize this truth, that things unfold from within outwards—that the world is guided from this inner plane.

> The whole world is animated and lit, down to its most material shapes, by a world within it. This inner world is called Astral by some people, and it is as good a word as any other, though it merely means starry; but the stars, as Locke pointed out, are luminous bodies which give light of themselves. This quality is characteristic of the life which lies within matter; for those who see it, need no lamp to see it by. The word star, moreover, is derived from the Anglo-Saxon "stir-an," to steer, to stir, to move, and undeniably it is the inner life which is master of the outer, just as a man's brain guides the movements of his lips. (Mabel Collins, *Light on the Path*)

If we really believed this truism, we would apply the same intensity as the cat to our vigil at the window of our souls. Our distractions are so strong and our watchfulness so tenuous, that the only way we can begin to develop an attunement to this inner knowledge and guide is to deliberately sit ourselves down in an environment of tranquility and silence. With practice, a sense of connection with this alternate reality begins to arise and we are drawn more often to that window—even at unscheduled times when the need arises. Within this wellspring of silence can arise the strength of being to dare and persist, the potentiality of inspiration to solve issues and create a better world, and the certainty of direction to guide us into our higher purpose.

As soon as we realize that these are the grand prizes dancing just beyond our reach through the window, one would think that we would become just as intense in our vigil as the cat, watching to catch the slightest hints from the world beyond the window— the world in which our higher self, our ultimate master, resides.

TOO MUCH OF A GOOD THING

"BE CAREFUL WHAT you wish for because you might just get it," we often hear. In the middle of July, we wish for cold, and in mid-February, we long for hot summer days. If we are suffering a drought, we long for rains, but in flood conditions we cannot bear to see any more rain. This also is true for rest and work, depending on whether we are fatigued or bored. And so the list goes on. We are rather like Goldilocks when tasting the three bears' porridge. Papa Bear's was too hot; Mama Bear's was too cold; but Baby Bear's was just right, not extreme in either direction.

There is truth to the saying that evil is an exaggerated virtue. Knowledge is good, but too much theory without practical understanding leads to either dullness or fanaticism. Balance and proportion are crucial for the welfare of the whole. Although the underlying unity of the cosmos is undeniable, the list of apparent opposites in this manifested universe is endless: pliable and rigid, dark and light, strength and gentleness, etc. The tension between these opposites holds the whole system together and provides the field for our consciousness and growth.

FATHER-MOTHER SPIN A WEB WHOSE UPPER END
IS FASTENED TO SPIRIT (*Purusha*)—THE LIGHT OF
THE ONE DARKNESS—AND THE LOWER ONE TO

MATTER (*Prakriti*), ITS (*the Spirit's*) SHADOWY END;
AND THIS WEB IS THE UNIVERSE SPUN OUT OF
THE TWO SUBSTANCES MADE IN ONE, WHICH IS
SWÂBHÂVAT (*self-becoming or unfolding out of itself*).
(*The Secret Doctrine*, Stanza III, sloka 10)

Our universe requires a dynamic and complementary tension between the opposite forces called yin and yang, as illustrated by the Chinese symbol. Each of the equally divided dark and light portions of the revolving circle contains a germ of the other within its segment, showing that each aspect depends on the presence of the other in their eternal cosmic dance.

These energies, yin/yang, female/male, receptive/assertive, negative/positive, etc., are a part of this grand drama in which we, as participants, have to figure out how to find harmony and balance. Each of us has both types of qualities, but manifesting as male or female; we express one or the other more strongly. Yet either quality requires the mitigating presence of the other. This is true within our selves as well as in society. Protective fortitude is as necessary as sustaining nurturance. Because the masculine aspect has been overemphasized for several millennia, today, the need for finding balance through increased appreciation for the feminine is gaining expression.

Consider the image of the potter and clay. Being the clay or material to be shaped unto a useful vessel, we have to undergo the molding process. So that we may contain the feminine aspect of receptivity, we are shaped into a hollow that is open to spirit. Yet our substance has to be strong and resistant enough (a masculine quality) to be able to form and maintain a sturdy shape. When the clay is too wet and soft to be worked, it will collapse in on itself and be unable to function as a vessel. A balance in strength and pliability is needed.

We cannot promote one aspect of our nature over another. We have to be receptive to divine spirit, but we also have to present robust material for the potter's use. Therefore we need to develop a self-responsible, self-reliant strength that does not crumble under whatever energy happens our way. In order to be whole in our development we require strength of identity and purpose, while at the same time maintaining a gentle receptivity. If one day, we are to serve as teachers and masters of wisdom, we need to balance equally the masculine and feminine qualities within.

The chalice, a symbol of the feminine because its concave shape provides it with a potential for being filled, has always been a part of the Christian tradition. In spite of its importance in the sacrament of communion, however, the chalice has not held a prominent place in religious iconography. Possibly the chalice's low visibility has been symptomatic of the Church's limited acknowledgement of the feminine.

In fact, the West's long love affair with the Arthurian grail legends may have been spawned by this lack of feminine empowerment. The stories abound with brave and gallant knights charging in quest of the elusive grail. Nevertheless, it turns out that it is not bravery which wins the goal, but a receptive, purity of heart. Moreover, woven throughout the tales of adventure are encounters with powerful women who must be reckoned with along the way. The knights were seeking and being challenged by the feminine.

In the Hindu tradition, we find another story which prompts the audience to rethink and honor the feminine. Long ago there was a young aspiring yogini who longed to be the disciple of a great teacher. She approached him several times but was not even allowed past his outer devotees. In spite of rebuffs and ridicule, she persisted and finally gained audience with him. He promptly dismissed her youthful enthusiasm with the pronouncement that he did not accept females as his students. After persistent suppli- cations on her part however, he accepted her argument that "all humanity must become feminine, or receptive, to divine spirit." He recognized in her argument a truth that resulted from an inner experience of wholeness and spiritual maturity.

Consideration of the feminine principle does not mean that we should promote one quality over the other, but that we should enhance that quality which has been most lacking in empowerment and acknowledgement. In doing so, we can achieve greater balance, in both our personal lives and in society around us. Equal appre- ciation of both qualities generates wholeness and encourages the full expression of humanity. Just as we would not choose to use only one eye, one leg, or one hand, so we should not choose to strengthen one of these aspects over another.

Whichever quality is less in your comfort zone is the one to pursue. Honor the receptiveness within your self, that you might be open to others, to nature, and to the Spirit that pours its power into our inner sanctuary; develop your strength of character, self-assertion, and action so that you might be of greater service to the world. Develop the mettle to hold the form, and the empti- ness to become the receptive hollow. Be whole in both weakness and strength.

In *Stories of the Spirit, Stories of the Heart*, edited by Christina Feldman and Jack Kornfield, on page 283, the following illustra- tion is given in a repertoire of the Dalai Lama's parables. Once, the spirit of a famous guru appeared in order to heal a small, discor- dant community of monks. All the monks had seen the spirit come out of the wall long enough to utter just one word. But each monk had heard a different word. The event is immortalized in this poem:

> The one who wanted to die heard *live*.
> The one who wanted to live heard *die*.
> The one who wanted to take heard *give*.
> The one who wanted to give heard *keep*.
> The one who was always alert heard *sleep*.
> The one who was always asleep heard *wake*.
> The one who wanted to leave heard *stay*.
> The one who wanted to stay, *depart*.
> The one who never spoke heard *preach*.
> The one who always preached heard *pray*.
> Each one learned how he had been
> In someone else's way.
>   Originally told by Pierre Delattre

That which makes us whole, will be neither too much nor too little, but just right.

OPEN WIDE THE GATES

IN THE VOLATILE region of the Middle East, what strange circumstance could result in a person of the Muslim faith being the gatekeeper for the Church of the Holy Sepulcher in Jerusalem, one of the holiest shrines in all of Christendom? Once again, we find that truth is stranger than fiction. Several years ago, the Associated Press told the story of Wajeeh Nuseibeh whose family has monitored those massive doors for more than a thousand years due to sectarian squabbling among the Christians.

A source of stability through centuries of discord has been an agreement made in 638 CE, between the conquering Muslim Caliph, Omar Ibn al-Khattab, and the Greek patriarch. In accordance with this agreement, a series of several families have assumed that gate keeping responsibility. The shrine, re-built by European crusaders in 1099, at the site purported to be the burial tomb of Jesus, has been the destination for holy pilgrimages of many different sects of Christianity since its earliest foundation. Yet, for the very reason that it is so revered, it continues to be a source of contention. Because many sects have had to share this most holy of sites, no one can agree as to who should maintain control. As recently as July 28, 2005, Coptic and Ethiopian monks engaged in rock-throwing and fighting over a perceived challenge of control over a courtyard in the shrine. Tensions run high among all the groups who want to worship there.

Only the long established ritual of gate keeping by our Muslim brothers maintains the peace. Every morning a Joudeh, another Muslim family who guards the ten inch iron key, hands the key to a Nuseibeh. Following his family tradition as he has done for the last twenty-five years, fifty year-old Wajeeh Nuseibah, then climbs a wooden ladder passed down by a priest from within the shrine, and opens the spring-loaded iron lock. Wajeeh has 400 year-old documents declaring his family's control of the gates, while the Joudeh family's management of the key dates back to the Ottoman rule, which began in 1517.

During the recent turmoil, the families have had to send surrogates to open the gates at four in the morning in order to avoid the dangers of the nighttime streets, but they still maintain enough control to keep peace among the various factions. Wajeeh says that these Muslim families act as a people of peace for the church.

Gates provide an access point. They are the way in and out. In the case of the Church of the Holy Sepulcher the gates control who goes in and out—and when. But just as importantly, gates also mark entry points. Gates provide the way to enter into another territory. The very presence of a gate indicates that there is more beyond. In our own lives we can see the importance of discovering the gate within that leads to deeper understanding.

Just as Wajeeh makes it possible for the Christians to enter the shrine in peace, each one of us can be a gatekeeper for Theosophy—not to keep people out (although by our poor example this may sometimes be the unintended result), but to indicate that there is an open door available to any earnest seeker. To the extent of our knowledge we can point out the way—the way to explore and grow in understanding, with abundant resources, which is unfettered by the narrowness of sectarian views. We can herald that entrance and hope that those who pass through on our watch will pay us the ultimate compliment for any teacher—that of surpassing us in knowledge and application of principles.

As Theosophists we may be cautious about giving out our views to others in any way that might be seen as proselytizing. In fact, we usually bend over backwards to be sure that we honor all approaches to religion and the riddles of life. This is as it should be if we are talking about imposing our views on others, but we have to face up to the awesome responsibility of sharing whatever level of understanding we have attained in order to benefit our fellows in this life journey. There are many people for whom our gate is virtually invisible unless we make it known.

Madame Blavatsky talks about this responsibility in *The Key to Theosophy*:

> ENQUIRER: Is it the duty of every member to teach others and preach Theosophy?
>
> THEOSOPHIST: It is indeed. No fellow has a right to remain idle, on the excuse that he knows too little to teach. For he may always be sure that he will find others who know still less than himself. And also it is not until a man begins to try to teach others, that he discovers his own ignorance and tries to remove it.

We might wonder, "How can I be a gatekeeper to point the way for others? What do I know that can point the way to the gate?" In notes from *Light on the Path*, the answer is given: "Hardness of heart belongs to the selfish man, the egotist, to whom the gate is for ever closed."

The gift of Theosophy is a worldview that forever shatters selfishness and hardness of heart. As given by Madame Blavatsky in *The Secret Doctrine*, the first fundamental principle takes us directly to the key for that gate. It states that there is one omnipotent boundless ALL, called God by some—and it leads us to an understanding that there is only one unitive principle within which all else, including ourselves, exists. If we take to heart this one factor, we will naturally open the gate within ourselves, and become a beacon to others.

We may not necessarily know the particular answers to another's questions, but with humility and open heart, we will be able to point the way. We can say, "There is a gate. Look inside and see if you find the way to the sense of completeness you seek." We can open wide the gate that will draw them toward their own inner truth.

LIVING WATERS

WHAT AN AMAZING feat it is to be able to send rockets to Mars! But not only that—we are also able to send robotic vehicles that relay pictures and scientific data about the surface rocks and subsoil. Recently, David and I had the privilege of attending one of the programs from the National Geographic Live! Series held at the Field Museum in Chicago. Films and narrative about the latest findings from Mars, our neighboring planet, were presented by Kobie Boykins, an engineer responsible for the solar panels used in the Mars Expedition rovers, Spirit and Opportunity.

One of their striking findings is that, in addition to the polar icecaps, there may have been large bodies of water on Mars. Many of the formations on the surface appear to be dried lake or ocean beds. If this is true, and Mars did indeed have vast amounts of water, where are the lakes or oceans now? Is what happened to the water something that could potentially happen to our own vast bodies of water?

Of course no one knows for sure, as our science in this area is in its infancy. Yet when we can explore the surface of the moon or another planet, it makes us realize afresh the great gift of our little space-island home and the importance of working in cooperation with all who share this habitation, that we might sustain it and flourish. This is the reverberating message of all who have explored space and our relative place in the solar system.

Because of stories, legend, and even some of our Theosophical writings, a big question in the minds of many has been, "Is there or could there have been life on Mars?" The identification of ice caps in the polar regions certainly indicates the presence of water, and now the identification of probable lake beds make it seem that there may have been vast amounts of water at some time in the distant past. The question of the presence of water is crucial because in our Earth's environment, wherever water is to be found, there is life. This is true for the deepest oceans around the hot and toxic fumaroles, the icy waters of the Arctic and Antarctic, as well as fresh water lakes, whether they be highly acidic, salty, or basic.

Water seems to be an essential element for life. It is the solvent in which minerals and proteins can combine and blend in order to build living forms. Even our bodies are composed of at least sixty percent water. Without the circulatory and lymphatic systems (our blood is eighty-three percent water), there would be no way to support the various chemical and biological processes necessary for life as a complex organism. The great solvent circulates chemical messages and nutrients, and washes away the wastes and impurities in such a way that the systems function as a cohesive whole.

In religious traditions and myths, water is used as a symbol for attaining a more meaningful life. If there is a desert, or dry and thirsty land, it is symbolic of a psychological state in which one feels empty or devoid of meaning. Jesus had to face his temptations in the desert. The Israelites had to wander in the desert for forty years before they could enter the Promised Land. And of course all of the lands around the avaricious dragon Smaug's lair, of Tolkien fame, were parched and barren.

Where there is water, however, the desert blooms and life flourishes in abundance. The holy Mt. Kailash in western Tibet is the traditional source of the four great rivers, the Ganges, Indus, Sutlej, and Brahmaputra, and as such is considered sacred by the Hindu, Buddhist, Jain, and Don religions. It is said to be the abode of the Hindu god Shiva.

The sacred lotus flower of the East, while having its roots in the physical earth and its blossom in the open sunlight, requires water to support its stem. If the mud represents the physical and the blossom in the open sunlight above is emblematical of spiritual enlightenment, then let us consider the meaning of the intervening water. The moisture of life seems to be related to consciousness, but not just any consciousness. Angry, violent, or selfish people are conscious, but they would be said to still be living in the desert.

The way to drink deeply of the living waters is to apply consciousness toward meaning and wholeness. Though not easily achieved, this can be accomplished incrementally by directing attention to the inner life, studying the works of sages, and being open to the insights that come from meditation. Slowly we can each cultivate our consciousness to become the living waters of compassionate unity. And gradually, as we learn to identify with a higher purpose, we breathe moisture around us to others who may also begin to wake up to a higher purpose.

Mars was known as the fierce god of war, and borne in that mythology is a truth for our instruction. Perhaps that warring energy is what turned his namesake planet into a desert, if it ever did support life forms. We should take note of the capability that we humans have to turn our unique garden spot in the solar system into a similar wasteland through our lack of concern for environmental issues and our bellicose and greedy natures. But the root causes lie within each of us as individuals. The moisture of the consciousness of each one of us, enlightened, or at least aiming in that direction, serves to water the gardens of earth and encourage the desert of our existence to flower.

In the Second Fragment of *The Voice of the Silence*, Madame Blavatsky compares this kind of consciousness to Amrita's clear waters, which are an essential ingredient in the bread of Wisdom. Maya's dew is the consciousness of hatred and selfishness.

> "Great Sifter" is the name of the "Heart Doctrine," O disciple. (v.120)

> The wheel of the good Law moves swiftly on. It grinds by night and day. The worthless husks it drives from out the golden grain, the refuse from the flour. The hand of Karma guides the wheel; the revolutions mark the beatings of the Karmic heart. (v. 121)

> True knowledge is the flour, false learning is the husk. If thou would'st eat the bread of Wisdom, thy flour thou hast to knead with Amrita's [immortality] clear waters. But if thou kneadest husks with Maya's dew, thou canst create but food for the black doves of death, the birds of birth, decay and sorrow. (v. 122)

> If thou art told that to become Arhan thou hast to cease to love all beings—tell them they lie. (v.123)

On a daily basis, consider your life and how you might add to the well-being of another; think of the beauty and treasures of this earth; explore the deep recesses of your heart for meaning and purpose in the realms of immortality. By doing so, each day you will be increasing the joy, gratitude, and understanding that fills our lives and our planet with living waters.

HOW DOES YOUR GARDEN GROW?

HOUSEPLANTS ARE A luxury that I have decided to do without due to the current state of my responsibilities. My days and weeks fly by so swiftly that I had to choose kindness to the plant kingdom over misplaced ambitions of providing regular care for individual plants. Houseplants are wonderful little green (for the most part) beings that provide a hominess and ambience, besides of course, their benefit to the environment in general. My mother, who has quite a green thumb, fills every vacant window space with the little darlings and thinks of them as her children. Although these small green living things require very little attention, that attention cannot be sporadic. Several weeks or a month of neglect can deal a fatal blow to the healthiest plant.

Consistency in applied spirituality serves the purpose of watering our seeds of aspiration. Just as good intentions alone do not provide the sustenance needed by the plant, so do our spiritual roots starve if we only prefer to think good thoughts without putting them into action. The exercise of the will to achieve, no matter how limited the actual contribution may appear on the physical plane, generates major currents in the spiritual waters of the world.

In other words, if it is easy for us to give a pittance to alleviate poverty now and again, then that act has provided very little sustenance for our soul. But, if we give generously from limited resources, as did the widow in Jesus' story concerning contributions in the temple, then our soul is nourished through that sacrificial act. Moreover, as in all teaching stories or parables, the symbolism points beyond the literal facts. The teaching applies to our way of life, not just to our pocketbooks. As the saying goes, time is money. Sympathetic attention and cultivation of a responsible attitude are valuables which also contribute to the whole.

So Theosophy demands an ethic higher than anything that can be defined in rules of conduct. It calls not for passive acquiescence, but rather an active involvement in recognizing our participation and contribution to the whole. Active service, according to our capacity and opportunity, is a necessary component of our spiritual health.

As Madam Blavatsky said in the second fragment of the *Voice of the Silence*, "Shalt thou abstain from action? Not so shall gain thy soul her freedom. To reach Nirvana one must reach Self-Knowledge, and Self-Knowledge is of loving deeds the child." Continuing with this thought elsewhere, she further stated that "The Theosophist who is at all in earnest, sees his responsibility and endeavours to find knowledge, living, in the meantime, up to the highest standard of which he is aware. (*Collected Writings*, Volume IX, p. 4–5)

Thus it is not the occasional act of service or valor that builds our spiritual foundation, but the regular care and watering of an altruistic attitude. Moment by moment the seed of our spirit is cultivated, so that it can develop and bloom in its own time. As long as we have breath we cannot give up. There is always someone or something which needs our attention.

Of course, we cannot lose sight of the fact that meeting karmic responsibilities and attending to one's own needs are a part of maintaining the overall health of the garden of life. But complacency, mediocrity, and discouragement compromise the quality of our garden's environment. There are so many small ways in which we can begin to reorient our attention.

As a simple example, consider the act of voting. Frustrating and inadequate or not, if this right is not exercised, what little voice we have in the affairs of government will disappear. Though we claim to be a model democracy, a recent survey of voting-age citizens showed that the United States ranked 139th out of 172 nations in voting participation (*Parade* Magazine, January 14, 2007). This does not speak well of our commitment to democratic principles.

We might further consider our random acts of kindness, or lack thereof, when we find ourselves behind the wheel in heavy traffic. Think of hidden prejudices and biases that may have crept into our attitudes which will eventually find their way into our relationships. In every act and attitude, we are either reducing the light and nutrients available to the flower of our soul, or we are tending it properly with the sustenance it needs.

An occasional ethically noble act is like an occasional watering of our philodendron and violets. It might, for a while, keep them from turning up their toes, but it will not allow them to flourish. A truly ethical person has incorporated authentic acts of kindness and justice into their very being. With this kind of regular care and watering, the soul exhibits amazing strength in overcoming adversity and unfolding its potential. As Tennessee Williams once said, "The violets in the mountains have broken the rocks."

How does your garden grow? With neglect and by happenstance, or with regular attention and active care?

TAKE A BITE

THOSE WHO GREW up with the Biblical tradition of Adam and Eve have often heard that they were born sinful because of Eve's actions. Eve took a bite of the fruit of the Tree of Knowledge of Good and Evil, and then convinced Adam to do the same—at the urging of the serpent, of course. Viewed allegorically, the story may speak of the coming of age for humanity, when intellectual acumen (the wisdom of the serpent) had reached the level which brought humankind to the age of accountability, that stage at which one becomes self-responsible and capable of understanding the difference between right and wrong.

From that point in our development, we humans have had the tendency to make poor choices and then to say, "The devil made me do it!" When things go awry we do not like to think that we may have done anything to cause the problem. We prefer to point the finger of blame in every direction but toward ourselves. And truly, it does seem that from birth we are caught up in a stream of circumstances that shape us in ways that tend to make us repeat the same mistakes again and again. Caught in our personality quirks and throes of our circumstances, we deny the presence of freewill, one of our greatest gifts and the tool by which we can begin our spiritual journey back to the source of our being.

We say that we are inextricably caught in a quagmire of

predestined events. Fate has had it in for us from the beginning, so now we will just continue as we have been and hope that something outside ourselves will intervene. Viewed from the perspective of the blind and struggling personality there is some truth to this view. At any moment in time, however, we have the freedom to reach into the deeper core of our being where abides will, purpose, and loving kindness. At such a moment everything shifts and we can catch a glimpse of the possibilities rather than the limitations. Madam Blavatsky wrote about freewill in relation to astrology but her statements apply equally to astrology, fate, or predestination.

> I hold, moreover, that astrology, being a calculation of the planetary influences on an individual, is merely a science of tendencies. In other words, the influences in themselves are such as to predispose the individual to adopt the line of action predicted. Man, however, being endued with what is called freewill, but what I prefer to call latent will-power or soul-power, may develop it to such an extent that he may successfully oppose the planetary influences and overcome what is popularly known as fate. It is only when the individual is passive, or when his will-power is undeveloped and feeble, or when, the will-power being developed, he works in the direction of the planetary influences themselves, that astrological predictions will be realized. Hence it is that we hear it said that when a person possessing the necessary amount of developed will-power is initiated into the mysteries of occultism, he passes beyond the pale of astrological predictions. (*Collected Works* vol. 6, 327)

Each of us does begin this life with a unique set of circumstances, tendencies, and talents. Whatever they are, we can make the most of them and even rise above them. We can turn them into opportunities for learning, service, and even joy—but only by changing our attitudes and directly facing the things we fear or dislike, by exercising our will power.

If this is true, why do we often feel so trapped as if there is no way we can make a difference? Perhaps our own timidity and fear is our greatest jailer. Freedom of will is available only to the bold. As American author and lecturer Marianne Williamson said, "Our deepest fear is not that we are inadequate. Our deepest fear is that we are powerful beyond measure. It is our Light, not our Darkness, that most frightens us." We have a vast potential that in our weaker-willed moments we tremble even to consider. Rather than shrinking away with feelings of unworthiness or inadequacy, claim your power to be all that you can be. Direct your energies toward the powers of love and life; be creative in seeing the opportunity in each challenge or failure. Take responsibility boldly, and see how your life begins to turn around, ever so slowly perhaps at first, but turn it will.

As your life changes, so does the rest of the world—one small step at a time. And the small steps of each of us toward wholeness and peace can and will transform the world. As Galadriel told Frodo in the *Lord of the Rings* trilogy, "Even the smallest person can change the course of the future. This is yours to do. No one else can do it for you" (*Lord of the Rings: The Fellowship of the Ring*, movie 2001).

Each of us is responsible of our own freewill to incorporate the fruit of the Tree of Knowledge of Good and Evil into our understanding and judgment so that we can fully claim its power. Take a big bite and then listen to the wisdom of the inner self and dare to follow where it leads. In doing so, you will claim the truth of freewill for yourself and begin to recreate the idyllic nature of the original Garden of Eden in the world around us. It is possible to move in that direction if enough of us recognize our precious birthright of personal responsibility. Used wisely, that power will transform the world. It is available to each of us for the choosing.

LIGHT AS A FEATHER

MY MORNING WALKS often yield tidbits for further contemplation. I relate to the Native American tradition that nature has many secrets to reveal if she is observed with sensitivity. Sometimes, it is just the inspiration of peace and beauty flowing gently into view. But at other times, an object or event triggers some specific insight, or at least fanciful meanderings that reveal a meaningful message.

On one particular morning, a startlingly large feather adorned my otherwise ordinary path of pebbles and weedy grass patches. Almost automatically, it found its way into my hand for further examination and contemplation. The feather was quite unremarkable except for its size—mostly black with indistinct striations of a brownish hue. For a feather to be so large, it must surely be essential for flying—either a large tail or wing feather.

Could the bird have been injured in a fight, perhaps protecting its nest? Or was it merely molting and had already grown a replacement? In either case, to try to catch the bird to return the lost item would be detrimental to all concerned. Once dislodged from its original location, its usefulness to the bird had ceased.

In being committed to helping a fellow human being, we might feel that we know just what they are missing and feel quite justified in attempting to place their seemingly missing feathers (or other qualities) just where we think they should go. Of course this is ridiculous for either a bird's feathers or a person's qualities.

Growth and healing can only be organic, arising from within. If we want to help another, we have to let go of our particular biases and tune into their circumstance and soul's essence. It might be called empathy, or a recognition of our essential unity with the other, but by whatever name, it is an essential quality for being able to benefit others.

Colonel Olcott recognized this when he immersed himself in improving the plight of the native born Buddhists in India, Sri Lanka, and other lands under the rule of European colonialists. He became one with them, working diligently to help them reclaim the religious tradition into which they were born and the dignity of their native culture. He expressed this empathy in the following statement in Volume II of *Old Diary Leaves*:

> The most difficult lesson for a white man in Asia to learn is, that the customs of his people and those of the dusky races are absolutely different, and that if he dreams of getting on well with the latter he must lay aside all prejudices and hereditary standards of manners, and be one with them, both in spirit and in external form. (382)

He recognized that he had to rid himself of his Western cultural prejudices in order to be in full harmony with the plights and needs of the people, and thus be able to render true assistance. With an understanding heart he was able to become one with them and work to help them from an inside perspective. Much to the amazement of the other colonists, the Colonel was accepted almost instantly into the homes and hearts of the native people.

This first step of fully empathizing is certainly an important one when trying to be of service, but there is another point of consideration that can be overlooked. In order to make a difference in the world, we, ourselves, must be whole—or at least be working in that direction. The feather also points to this important lesson. When helping another, we have to be careful not to pull out our own feathers in the process. If we damage ourselves, our usefulness to others is greatly diminished. A bird which has lost some of its feathers surely cannot fly as fast. In fact, birds are far more vulnerable during the molting season. To assure that we do not lose the feathers of our being, we always have to remember to nurture the core of our being. The basic principle underlying our beneficial effectiveness is an attitude of wholeness which grows out of an inner connection with our higher nature.

This wholeness results from recognizing and cultivating our own spiritual needs, taking into account all aspects of our lives, health, responsibilities, circumstance, and relationships. Each one of us has to discover the meaning of wholeness for ourselves as we explore the unity of all life and our place within that wholeness. We have to find the balance point in which we can be the cup that is never empty, always giving, but always filled again. HPB cautioned us to maintain this balance point in *The Voice of the Silence*:

> Beware, lest in the care of Self thy Soul should lose her foothold on the soil of Deva-knowledge.
> Beware, lest in forgetting SELF, thy Soul lose o'er its trembling mind control, and forfeit thus the due fruition of its conquests.

The study and mediation that we Theosophists are exhorted to do is a part of that process of educating ourselves for more balanced and effective action. Action which springs from this center will be more useful and less tiring. In fact, when done well and in harmony with ourselves and our world, it can be energizing. This sounds easy, but it is a process of constant learning and readjustment. Service to others flows out of a concern for their well-being, but we can become so immersed in trying to help that we often forget our own needs. As I can attest, the self is an ingredient never to be forgotten or it will call attention to itself in most inconvenient ways. When one is fatigued, one cannot be as effective, and things can oft go awry.

We can, however, keep the goal before us, and at the very least, have the intention to nurture ourselves as we nurture others. Moreover, besides the usual physical needs, we also have a deep spiritual need for meaning and purpose. So it follows that performing action for the benefit of others completes the circle of a meaningful existence, which restores the soul.

When seen in this way, service can become the joy of living, not the drudgery. It can flow from a balanced heart full of understanding and compassion. There may be and most probably will be some sacrifices required along the way, but these are the sacrifices of lesser pleasures and self-centeredness. To unburden ourselves of these things brings a kind of lightness to life. As we learn to give from an inner abundance, we may discover that work performed in service can feel as light as a feather.

THE POWER OF THE WATER BEARER

WE HEAR SO MUCH about the dawning of the Age of Aquarius, but many of us do not have a clue as to what that means. Aquarius is represented by the water bearer pouring forth the waters of wisdom, and marks a time in which energy is defined by the term, "I know." According to astrologers (among whose numbers I cannot count myself), as we follow the sidereal progression of the equinoxes, we are moving from the Piscean age, expressed as a focus on faith and orthodoxy, to the Aquarian expression of a more open-minded attitude based on experiential knowledge combined with the energy of group work. In other words, whereas we have been oriented to individual belief, we will now be moving toward cooperative group work within the context of individual understandings.

In the midst of all the turmoil our world is currently experiencing related to rigid beliefs and orthodoxy, or fundamentalist thinking, the hope of an influx of cooperative and open-minded energy is definitely encouraging. When the founders began the Theosophical Society, they introduced an early impetus for change to a world caught in the throes of a mechanical materialistic view on the one hand and an imperialistic, belief-structured orthodoxy on the other. The founders wrought the great experiment, called the Theosophical Society, in order to popularize the wisdom traditions and to stimulate humanity's awareness of its universal kinship—to move thinking from the narrow to a broader perspective.

The Aquarian idea of life-giving wisdom and compassion is an age-old concept and has been symbolized in traditions other than astrology. Kwan Yin is represented as a deity, who tips a vial of the precious elixir of life so that the droplets are available to nourish all. In this form she is also considered to be the oriental feminine version of Avalokiteshvara, or the Buddha of compassion. Pouring out pitchers of water, the kneeling figure in the Star card of the Major Arcana Tarot represents seeking and sharing wisdom in the depths of the psyche. Although free flowing water tends to represent our emotional natures, water contained or controlled by a vial or pitcher seems to represent those emotions contained and controlled by a higher faculty in order to provide wisdom. Notice that the wisdom is not static but is shared with humanity.

The challenge of the water bearer is to be able to contain the emotional nature in a healthy way. One has to find wholeness within oneself in order to function most effectively and freely in cooperation, without being swallowed up or losing one's independence and individuality in the group. Being able to achieve this balance is a major task set before us.

I have always loved science fiction as a vehicle for divulging some of the otherwise barely communicable mysteries of life. One such story is told in *Stardance* by Spider Robinson. I read it a long time ago, but it transmitted to me a powerful image. As I remember, the story begins with a rather gray, mundane life on planet Earth, where the various characters' lives are separate, colorless, and barely manageable. Yet the threads of events bring them all to be inhabitants of a space station on the outer edges of our planetary system.

As they weather various difficulties, they learn to cooperate and synchronize with each other in a freeform, non-gravitational field. Developing their individual talents and contributing to the whole, enables them to gradually unfold empathetic psychic connections with one another. When they have reached a culmination in their harmonious interactions, a rapidly approaching frightful menace appears in the far distant space. The out-posted characters realize that they must figure out how to stop this threat in order to save themselves and their civilization still on Earth.

As the fiery globe, swirling with vibrant energy, approaches, the characters' heightened sensitivity allows them to intuit that this terrible consciousness may be subject to some sort of reason or appeasement. In the end, the characters discover that they are like this amazing space entity—which, though one entity, is yet a composite of many beings who buzz and vibrate together like a huge beehive. This composite being is drawn to the presence of this little pod of humanity which has begun to function as a unit, sensing each others' needs and actions, and caring enough about each other to sacrifice self for the whole. In so doing, they have reached the next developmental stage and are ready to move on as nurslings of a new order.

Although the weavings of the story are fascinating in themselves, the value of the story is in the message. Teilhard de Chardin tried to express the same idea in his description of the *noosphere*, that field of unified planetary consciousness in which we can all participate by lifting our hearts and minds to the Highest.

Although today's tragedies of terrorism and the uncertainties of global financial institutions are causes for deep concern, they can be viewed as the growing pains of an emerging larger community. Blurred political and economic boundaries challenge our many cultures to find new ways of honoring their individual identities, while at the same time developing peaceful ways to overlap with each other. Whether national groups or individuals, their collective attitudes color the psychic atmosphere and determine the potential welfare and level of peace for the whole planet.

For our part as individuals, we can recognize our responsibility for our own attitudes and spirit of cooperation. We can work to grow in personal strength in order to be fit vessels for the flow of compassion and wisdom. As we do so, the opportunities to join in creative cooperation with others will abound. Certainly the Theosophical Society is particularly suited to channeling group efforts toward supportive community, interfaith understanding, and intercultural cooperation. However we direct our efforts, together we are to be the water bearers, containing our experience with wisdom, and radiating our compassion with effectiveness. What greater human power can there be?

> For those who win onwards there is reward past all telling—the power to bless and save humanity. . . (*Collected Writings of Madame Blavatsky* XIII, 219)

IS A PUZZLEMENT

I LIKE PUZZLES: Sudoku, word jumbles, crosswords (if not too obscure), and picture puzzles. For some reason I particularly enjoy the multicolored patterns of different shapes and sizes in picture puzzles. Pictures with irregular edges or homogenous colors are particularly challenging, but provide great satisfaction as the pieces fit neatly together and progress has been made. The puzzle comes together painstakingly at first, slowly, ever so gradually. But as the pieces come together, the patterns emerge and the pile of missing pieces dwindles, the pace picks up. Finds become easier and easier until the last piece is in place.

The puzzle boxes usually proclaim something like: "750 pieces, all different." Think what confusion would ensue if there were several exactly the same shape. The more pieces exactly alike, the less satisfying the working of the puzzle would become. Each piece has a unique place in the picture, filling the exact grooves and matching with its neighbors. A single piece can be the key to finding other pieces, however, if one piece is missing, the puzzle cannot be completed and is usually discarded as useless.

Each one of us can be likened to a piece in the puzzle of life. We are each unique in shape, size, pattern, and fit. When we are jumbled out in the world, trying to make ourselves fit in where we are ill at ease, there does not seem to be any reasonable pattern to our discordant life. But, one day some bit of magic occurs and we find a neighboring piece—a kindred spirit who, through friendship, can play a part in the process of our spiritual growth. This usually results in several connections so that a cluster may be found.

Now it is true that sometimes, what seems like a good fit really is not, and so the trial and error may continue. But at some point we know we have found the peace of connecting into our spiritual home. Once in a while we may be jarred loose for some reason or other, but in the long run, we know where we belong.

Contact with another person (maybe even through the written word) is usually the catalyst that draws us, as social animals, to find our place in relation to others. The saying that no one is an island speaks a truth about humanity. Although essential to the whole, one may feel like an isolated piece on the edge of an irregular shape and out of sorts until the pattern falls into place.

Of course, the analogy goes only so far. Life is fluid and multidimensional. We are constantly changing, as are those around us, but our uniqueness is valuable to the whole. The cluster of our particular patterning —religious, cultural, professional, or personal—is essential for completing the rich fullness of human expression. We are important and our relationships to others are important.

To carry this metaphor a bit further, I will share a story from my childhood. An elderly neighbor had given my mother a little figurine of a child standing beside a baby carriage in a prayerful position. Being a little girl of maybe seven or eight who was particularly fond of dolls and baby carriages, I was always attracted to this little figure, but knew that I was not supposed to touch this fragile treasure. Well, I not only liked dolls, but also tended to get into my share of trouble. So the inevitable happened. I touched; it broke. I felt so bad about it that I gathered together every one of the twenty or so fragments, determined that I would fix it. For the better part of an afternoon, armed with Duco Cement, a newspaper surface, and diligent patience, I stayed out of any additional trouble by painstakingly reconstructing the figure.

Over the years that was one of Mother's most prized possessions. As it was always positioned in a place of honor, I was gratified to know that I had saved such a valuable piece. It was only years later that I learned it was not of monetary value after all, but that the latticework of yellowed lines of glue that crisscrossed the entire piece represented to my mother a loving daughter who had invested many a penitent hour in order to preserve something deemed important. The traces of glue gave it value beyond words.

The glue that binds us together as fellow travelers in our spiritual journey is the precious gold of the alchemists. Different though we may be, we become more precious as we join together in harmony, bound by mutual respect and love. Step by step, piece by piece, we find our unique place by connecting with and serving others.

Madam Blavatsky, in *Collected Writings* vol. VI, said of the Masters that: "The highest interest of humanity, as a whole, is their special concern, for they have identified themselves with that Universal Soul which runs through Humanity, and he, who would draw their attention, must do so through that Soul which pervades everywhere" (240). She states that our purposes are intricately bound with helping and healing humanity in its deepest heart. If we want to be in tune with the highest purposes for which the Society was founded, then we need to recognize our soul-connections with our brothers and sisters.

If this is true, why do we, who are committed to the spiritual path, often presume an overblown importance of our particular identity that translates to "My way or the highway?" Do we not know that the path requires a healthy dose of loving kindness every step of the way? How can we even imagine that the path is trod by seeking glamour for the self, intellectual pride, or indifference to the plight of others? As the King said to Anna in *The King and I*, "Is a puzzlement."

Our thoughts and actions this day can be the glue that begins to put a shattered figure like Humpty Dumpty back together again, through active involvement in appreciating and resolving differences among our brothers and sisters.

TREASURE HUNT

WHEN WE WERE children we had a game called a snipe hunt. The game could be played only once on the unwary victim who was stationed in a spot off the beaten path. This "victim" was then told to stay there holding a bag in order to catch the snipe that the rest would be stalking. We were supposed to chase the snipe into the waiting bag. Of course there was no snipe and finally the victim would catch on and come to look for the rest of us who were giggling and playing not too far off. As this is a very old game, it was seldom successfully carried out but was gleefully contemplated as a way of dealing with whoever was considered the neophyte at the time.

A far better variation of this game was a scavenger hunt, in which all were equally given a list of items to be found or "scavenged" in the area. There was the same opportunity to experience the joy of running around in the outdoors, but with no one being left out. All had the same challenge, but they were individual challenges with each individual or team pitted against all the others.

The next step up was the true treasure hunt, in which a map was provided for each or all to explore the territory using the map until the goal was found. Some maps were easier to read than others but "X" always marked the spot where treasure might be found. Although there are all kinds of variations, in the instance I remember, "X" marked the location where refreshments and equal treasure were shared by all. This kind of treasure hunt fits well with an analogy that I would like to draw.

The first instance is the way that we usually begin our spiritual pilgrimage. Everyone else seems to "get it" but we are at a loss as to what it is all about. We just know that there must be something more and so we are liable to do the bidding of some less-than-enlightened teachers. Although our search at this stage can be frustrating, it is a time of learning and growing. Once we see the fallacy of this passive approach, we realize the importance of being active participants. Someone else will not do it for us, but we have to do it ourselves. As Madam Blavatsky admonished in the Proem to *The Secret Doctrine* (I-17):

> In other words, no purely spiritual Buddhi (divine Soul) can have an independent (conscious) existence before the spark which issued from the pure Essence of the Universal Sixth principle,—or the OVER-SOUL,—has (a) passed through every elemental form of the phenomenal world of that Manvantara, and (b) acquired individuality, first by natural impulse, and then by self-induced and self-devised efforts (checked by its Karma), thus ascending through all the degrees of intelligence, from the lowest to the highest Manas, from mineral and plant, up to the holiest archangel (Dhyani-Buddha). The pivotal doctrine of the Esoteric philosophy admits no privileges or special gifts in man, save those won by his own Ego through personal effort and merit throughout a long series of metempsychoses and reincarnations.

Now this is a pretty heavy statement for those of us who have been hoping we could just rock along with business as usual, believing in various "good things," and that that would be sufficient for the nurture of our soul. Not so, says Blavatsky. We have to determine within ourselves how to re-orient our lives toward understanding our purposes in this world and to live every day by that highest understanding.

In this initial phase, we have an idea about some of the things we are looking for, but the instructions tend to be vaguely generic. We might look in a variety of places, gathering bits of treasure here and there. Although this wide casting about may seem like a waste of time, it truly is not. We grow and deepen through every effort to discover the ultimate treasure, and either slowly or quickly we come to the realization that a search oriented to the outer world will never bring us the true treasure. And the closer we come to glimpsing the treasure, the more we are drawn to approach it as the moth is drawn to the flame.

At this point we reach a new level in our quest. It becomes an almost effortless effort. Now all the random searching has borne its fruit and some inner guidance begins to flower within our being. No matter what tradition or religion we are following, there is a universal thread of truth (often called the ancient wisdom) which will draw us onto the path of no return—the path in the pathless land. Blavatsky (CW XIII 219) refers to it this way:

> I can tell you how to find those who will show you
> the secret gateway that opens inward only, and closes
> fast behind the neophyte for evermore.

We have received the map and it is written on our hearts in such a way that, though we may from time to time stray, we can never fully forget. In this treasure hunt, even more than there being no competition, there is a universal teamwork. When any one of us gains an additional insight into the treasure, we all profit from that experience. Humanity as a whole is blessed by the presence of an advancing soul. And the beauty of it is that by our alignment with this cosmic treasure hunt we are able to take part in the blessing of all humanity, no matter how humbly placed we may be. Blavatsky further explains this in *The Voice of the Silence*:

> 155. If Sun thou can'st not be, then be the humble planet. Aye, if thou art debarred from flaming like the noon-day Sun upon the snow-capped mount of purity eternal, then choose, O Neophyte, a humbler course.
> 156. Point out the "Way"—however dimly, and lost among the host—as does the evening star to those who tread their path in darkness.

As Theosophists we not only have the great gift of a treasure map, but also of being given the privilege of sharing with others the joy to be found in seeking the treasure. By being an evening star for our brother or sister, we discover the greatest treasure of all—that of realizing the unity of all life and forming a nucleus of the universal brotherhood of humanity.

ALONG THE WAY

HOW WOULD WE cope with the extreme altitudes 14,500 to 16,500 feet above sea level? Would we experience a major spiritual insight? Who were these folks we were going to spend the next two to three weeks with? These questions buzzed through our heads as we prepared for the journey to Tibet and again, as we began gathering at our rendezvous point in Beijing.

In the past, I have related to the word "pilgrimage" in terms of this lifetime of effort and unfoldment. Madame Blavatsky's description in the "Proem" of *The Secret Doctrine* rang true to my heart when I read of the obligatory pilgrimage of every soul "through the Cycle of Incarnation (or "Necessity") in accordance with Cyclic and Karmic law." It made sense that each struggling soul had its own purpose, challenges, and pathway. And we were each called upon to unravel the mystery for ourselves—with a little help from our friends, of course.

The other meaning of "pilgrimage," that of a particular physical journey in this world in order to visit a holy site, consistently applied to other people but not to me. There were a few destinations that could be termed loosely as pilgrimage sites, such as my regular treks during the 1980s to Stil-Light Theosophical Retreat Center in the Great Smoky Mountains, or my annual Thanksgiving homecomings to visit family in North Carolina; but these were journeys to familiar places with familiar people. The idea of pilgrimage as a journey to an unknown holy site with unknown people had not entered my personal experience until I joined the pilgrimage to Tibet.

We were well into the journey before I began to realize that the process of the journey was of equal importance to reaching the destination itself. Each obstacle we encountered provided an opportunity to bond with fellow pilgrims. Each holy site, reverent practitioner, or resting stopover made an important contribution to the whole. This process, supported by the mutual intent of each wayfarer, was the pilgrimage.

We did not come together merely to experience travel, or to see sights, but to gather nuggets of understanding and to encounter transformative inspiration. I do not know what we expected, but our first encounters with the Chinese in Tiananmen Square put us a little off balance. First, there was the friendliness of the people—they were particularly attracted to Chris Bolger's 6 foot 6 inch frame, but there was also an otherworldliness about the street vendors hawking English versions of the sayings of Chairman Mao, and the stark reality of several acres of open pavement broken only occasionally by a light pole, monument, or military guard stand. Shades of oppression nibbled at our peripheral vision.

Then, after a visit to the Lamasery, which sadly had been reduced to not much more than museum status, we were further introduced to the very different mindset of the Chinese government. Because of the Security Police's suspicions of Westerners in general, spiritually inclined travelers in particular, and a technical difficulty with one person's passport, our passage to Tibet was to be blocked. Skillful but tedious negotiations on the part of our guides finally resolved the issue with only one sacrificial lamb. Vicki Jerome of New Zealand would be barred from entry but would be compensated with her own private tour of holy sites, including the birthplaces of Tsongkapa and the Dalai Lama, in the former Amdo Province of Tibet, now known as Qinghai by the Chinese. Already we were confronted with unpleasant circumstances to accept and work around.

After a few days of acclimation in Beijing, we welcomed our flight to Lhasa which is located 14,000 feet above sea level, but we were all concerned about how we would react to the effects of high altitude. We had different remedies, mostly diuretics to give our fluidic circulating systems a jumpstart in order to function at the more rapid pace required by high altitude. We compared notes, shared our miseries, and generally adapted very well—all, that is, except for Valerie Malka from Australia who required extra pressurization/decompression in a portable body bag brought along for the occasion. Our guides, Glenn Mullin and Pawan Tuladhar, had thought of everything.

Every day was a new adventure of hiking, sitting, riding, eating, and settling into new accommodations—not to mention our creative toileting experiences. For our comfort breaks off the bus out on the open plateaus of Tibet, we were told, "Gents to the left; ladies to the right." Ladies were provided umbrellas for a modicum of modesty, but we soon found that it was easier to maneuver ourselves behind deep trenches or retaining walls. Eating establishments were usually ornately decorated, second floor, family style affairs. Most destinations were at the top of a mountain after an extended bus trip. Every aspect of physical life took care and attention. Nothing was according to the old routine. In having to break with our set patterns, we were finding enhanced capabilities and a new openness in ourselves.

During each adventure, we counted noses numerous times to be sure we were not missing anyone, but it was not always failsafe.

123

Once, after stopping at an outlook at one of the highest passes we traversed, we all clambered back on the buses and headed down the other side, glad to be out of the chill wind. All of a sudden the shout went up, "Where is John Besse?" The bus slowed down as we looked at the sight back up the road. John was running after the bus for all he was worth. We could not imagine a more desolate place to be marooned.

As bus mates, we sang, told jokes and stories, and shared intimate details, and were not unlike the pilgrims of Chaucer's *The Canterbury Tales.* Being thrown together in all sorts of circumstances brought about unusual opportunities to bond with fellow travelers on a mutual mission. These connections opened our hearts a bit wider and created new channels for caring communication within our psyches.

Not only did we get to know each other, but we developed an understanding and concern for our Tibetan brothers and sisters. We wrangled with them in the Free Market at Shigatse and believe me, when their very livelihood depends on the bargaining, they can be quite persistent. If one enters into the argument over pricing, one had better be prepared to make the purchase. After that point, "No" is not an acceptable answer. Later, we were most kindly served yak butter tea by the nuns at Ani Sangkhu Nunnery (a little sip will do you) and shared our western hats and clothing with gently curious native people. Our pilgrimage expanded our horizons and concerns for our fellow human beings in the larger world.

The underlying key to all of this, however, is the single spiritual focus—in this case that of touching the mystery of Tibet and its ancient teachings. A journey becomes a pilgrimage when the traveler, recognizing the purpose embedded in spiritual experience and unfoldment, becomes a pilgrim. With the help of our guides, we sought out the caves where great lamas achieved enlightenment, circumambulated holy temples (long the site of devotional destinations), mindfully turned the prayer wheels, hung prayer flags, and tossed the prayer papers called windhorses to the winds. And we meditated, meditated, meditated. Glenn provided rich explanations along the way and on occasion he or other monks would chant the sacred and timeless chants associated with Tibetan Buddhist practice.

Individual devotion and the power of place contributed to the tangible spiritual cohesiveness that developed over the course of the trip. Each precious temple or cave and each breathtaking mountain vista in the crisp clear air added its essence to the overall experience. The combined energy of the group enhanced the deep spiritual impact of our journey. The power of spiritual intention supported by fellow pilgrims and powerful places worked its magic on each of us, making a permanent impact on our being.

This rambling tale reveals the aspects of pilgrimage, whether as the one we made to Tibet last May, or the one on which we have embarked as an obligatory pilgrimage of the soul. The destination is not always crystal clear, but in order to make progress, the purpose must be set. In our personal pilgrimage, which is life itself, we have to cultivate our capabilities, be open to change, and deal with constraints and absolute obstacles. The joy and growth is to be found in rising to the challenges, growing in personal strength, supporting and being supported by others of like mind. The goal may recede as we approach it, but we are headed in the right direction if we cultivate and share our aspirations and care for one another along the way.

THE LIGHT OF THE WORLD

SUNLIGHT STREAMING THROUGH beautiful stained glass windows fills my earliest memories of religious or devotional feelings. Sitting in my family's regular Sunday morning pew and understanding little of what was going on, I would gaze at those luminous pictures of a loving shepherd holding the little lamb in his arms, or a kindly bearded man knocking to be given entry at a door draped with bunches of grapes. There was no shortage of beautiful church music and, on occasion after communion, the choir would gather around the altar rail and sing "The Lord Bless You and Keep You."

These experiences were outside the realm of my intellectual analysis, but they deeply imprinted on my heart a spiritual connection with the "other" that was not particularly conscious but a constant background presence. It did not make me religious, or even good, for that matter. In fact, "mischief" was said to be my middle name. However, in times of trouble or uncertainty the interior connection was a very present support. These experiences provided a mysterious access to an inner world that otherwise might have been invisible to me.

Depending on the individual, there are many different reactions to this weekly ritual, ranging from total boredom and resentment to conscious and life-changing inspiration. A few poignant symbols, connected and well presented, have the potential of striking an inner chord and mysteriously calling forth an intuitive response. Although unpredictable to some extent, the presence of inspiration is dependent on beauty, intentionality, and heart.

Beauty and culture were the two elixirs to humanity's evils identified by Nicholas Roerich in his writings. He felt that beauty had a unique way of speaking to one's soul and drawing out the best. Plato also identified Beauty as one of the trio of divine attributes along with the Good and the True. Although it is true that beauty is in the eye of the beholder, there is a certain balance and harmony within the form one might call beautiful that creates a sense of pleasure, and gives a certain lift to the spirit.

But beauty alone does not have transformative power. Perhaps this is why Roerich felt the need to include culture as one of the essential attributes for saving humanity. Intentionality, or understanding, has to imbue the beautiful with meaning so that some message of inspiration is transmitted. In this context the beauty is not for its own sake but is like the finger pointing at the moon, useful but not the end goal in itself, lest it become a hollow mockery. Inherent within the beauty of a sunset is a sense of awe and vastness of the whole of creation, thus inspiring the viewer to think beyond the small self.

The most important element, however, is what I call heart—the light of spirit which is a unitive, all-encompassing love. It is like the sunshine that streams through the many-colored windows to translate the darkened glass into colorful images. This spiritual light has the power to shine through and transform elements of this world from empty idols into icons or symbolic representations of a greater reality. Meaningful symbols or symbolic actions are, as expressed in the Book of Common Prayer of the Episcopal Church, outward and visible signs of inward and spiritual grace.

I mention the Christian idiom because that is my religion of birth and choice, but the use of symbols is universal to all religious traditions. Symbolic transmission of knowledge, in whatever system, is a gift for our human unfoldment. We have the unique ability to look into a metaphor and to see beyond it into unspoken truths. For this reason the preferred transmission of religious teachings has always been in metaphor and symbol. Certainly Madame Blavatsky chose the obscure and poetic Stanzas of Dhyzan as the foundational structure for her opus magnum, *The Secret Doctrine.*

As products of a materialistic, scientific age, we sometimes might forget the efficacy of using our inner light to look into and appreciate the subtleties of a symbolic or ritualistic approach to gaining insight into reality. Each of us would do well to draw to ourselves those symbols that inspire and encourage us. Moreover, we might remember that our regular practice of using them imbues them with the energy and power of heart and spiritual light. Each grain of practice helps to build a mountain of experience.

Yet, with routine and familiarity, we may forget the original inspiration. In fact, the one real danger in the use of symbols for our spiritual nurture is that we might lose sight of their true nature, getting lost in their outer forms, rather than drawing on the power of their beauty with intentionality and heart. But with conscientious effort we will access our inner light and, in the finding of it, develop a luminosity that becomes a beacon of hope for others.

In the afterword to *Esoteric Christianity*, Annie Besant inspires us to seek the mystery veiled in allegory in order that we might kindle our lights of intuition when she writes:

[We] have only lifted a corner of the Veil that hides the Virgin of Eternal Truth from the careless eyes of men. The hem of her garment only has been seen, heavy with gold, richly dight with pearls. Yet even this, as it waves slowly, breathes out celestial fragrances—the sandal and rose-attar of fairer worlds than ours.

BUTTERFLIES ARE NOT FREE

THE DRIFTING DAZZLING beauty of a butterfly wafting on the summer breezes, floating from flower to flower, conjures in us an aesthetic appreciation and a certain longing to be carefree like this diaphanous illusion. As the Buddhist teachings affirm, "All beings wish to be happy." And we human beings add the strength of our highly developed mental and emotional faculties to this search for happiness as a driving factor in our lives.

What can make us happy? After our basic needs are met, we begin to seek in all sorts of places. Thrills, power, and wealth might be pursued as the key to a sense of satisfaction. When the sense of meaning, purpose, and love are missing from our lives, our psyche can drive us into strange and self-destructive places. The things we long for the most are those things that are our half-remembered birthright. Our inner nature calls to us and tells us that we are so much more than this crazy merry-go-round in the physical world.

We are like the grub or caterpillar, pushing around in the dark, earthbound and prickly. We eat, we sleep, and we gather experiences, but an inner sense keeps nagging at us. Something important is missing. We begin weaving the web of self-examination—around and around, back and forth, until we might feel that there is nothing but darkness in our cocoon. In the process of this transformative pain, our insides can turn to mush. Nothing fits the old mold. What we might have thought was real and important is no longer so.

Whether this psychological alteration is long or short depends on many factors, but it must come in some way to each of our lives, turning ourselves inside out so that we no longer focus on self-pity and indulgences, but begin to recognize the fundamental unity with all of existence. Even the faintest glimmer of this realization begins to alter our nature that our wings of flight are just a breath away. It will not be long until we break free of our cocoon, fly into the sunlight of compassion, and sip the nectar of meaning in unity.

The butterfly is born, but not without a price. The process of change brings it to a state of amorphous chaos in which nothing seems certain. Yet in the unfoldment of time and under the condition that nothing goes awry, the lovely creature emerges in all its glory.

This imagery applies to the path of each human spirit in that we have undergone long development as self-protective, self-interested beings focused solely on our survival, who finally, through difficulties of one sort or another, have been catapulted into ourselves in order to grow beyond our accustomed boundaries. This happens cyclically within each life and on a grander scale through many lifetimes. Each new birthing is an initiatory experience along our return pathway to the divine nature hidden within, the only source of true happiness.

Because the pattern of development is so different for each of us in the way that it manifests, I might add an additional allusion to the butterfly. That is, "If a butterfly flutters its wings in China, there will be a powerful hurricane in the Atlantic." The truth of this phenomenon, which is called "sensitive dependence upon initial conditions" by chaos theorists, becomes more apparent daily as the internet and ever-increasing mobility exponentially expand our realms of influence. Each person's pathway has different circum-stances, so that there are as many pathways to Spirit as there are people. Together we are forming this lovely pattern of emerging butterflies. And we each impact untold others.

It is well to remember that the Theosophical Society in its many national sections, as well as the international Society as a whole, is a conglomerate entity which follows this same sort of pattern. We are blessed more than many organizations by the solid foun-dation of our long history. Yet it is clear that the further back into time our beginnings reach, the more transformational processes we will have to undergo to fulfill our mission as we develop and the world changes.

The Society has recently undergone an international election, unleashing controversy that disturbs us all—and that to some may seem like a step backward. However, it is by virtue of our func-tioning as a group, buffeting against one another elbow to elbow, that our prickles are shorn and our predispositions dissolved. As a microcosm of the entire human family we must learn to develop our own strengths while at the same time honoring our fellows undergoing the same process. Our interactions with one another create the environment and feedback that replicate the idea of a cocoon on a larger basis. Our self-focus and personal agendas must undergo radical change. With the necessity of looking into one another's eyes we are made to see ourselves more clearly, so that through a more lucid consciousness we are transformed and thus able to participate in building a more effective nucleus of the universal brotherhood of all.

It is neither simple nor easy, but our work as a Society draws each of us into the chaos of transformation and thereby recreates us to be contributing parts of the larger whole. By working together we bring about change in ourselves, from being selfishly ground-based caterpillars into the winged creatures of selfless service. Just as the individual has to experience trials and setbacks as a part of growth, so also the Society has to undergo the trauma of changes. To become a butterfly is difficult and is not free, but it is worth it.

After a contentious election in 1954, Sidney Cook, National Vice President, wrote:

> What is tremendously important is that after any electoral event in the Theosophical Society there be a renewal of our sense of oneness. So deep is the knowledge of our brotherhood—it is the very foundation cement of our Society's being—that when the partisanship ceases the true nature of our brotherly relationship and purpose again comes rapidly to the surface and directs our deliberations, our decisions and our actions. . . . Here lies the real test. It is in our groups, lodges, committees, boards, that our deepest principle must most evidently prevail. It is there we become or fail to become the nucleus upon which the whole welfare of the Society rests and upon which its whole vital work must be based. There can be no understanding of the Wisdom, no comprehension of the work without it.
>
> Now that the exaggerations of difference, fanned during an election, have disappeared, let the enthusiasm of our brotherhood possess us. (*American Theosophist*, August 1954, p. 150)

THE BALANCING ACT

ALTHOUGH MANY FORCES, including our own innate inclinations, draw us toward entering the path of spiritual growth, we can be daunted by the scary prospect before us. Who would want to walk the straight and narrow way without first having some idea of what may be entailed? It does not leave much room for error and sounds quite grueling.

The narrow way, or what has been called the razor-edged path, can be likened to a tightrope. Circus performers and other acrobats develop an amazing skill on the high-wire. Their skill requires long hours of practice and a keen development of the ability to focus on the task at hand. In fact, they are so trained to the precision performance that if there is any slip it is most likely due to a momentary loss of focus. As soon as the ego whispers, "Look at me; see how great I am," the performance is at risk of going awry.

For the spiritual path as well as the tightrope performance, a clear and directed consciousness is an essential element. This kind of steady focus breathes in the rarified air of dispassionate self-forgetfulness. It is not developed in a vacuum but unfolds over time in incremental steps of increasing difficulty. To begin with, we are more like children balancing on a line or crack in the pavement. There is no risk and it is more like a game of exploration than an actual practice. This is the stage of unconscious development. But consciousness is an amazing thing. It draws us forward as we gain control. We want to know; we want to grow. Growth begets growth.

Once there is a conscious desire for growth, we are confronted with a primary paradox of needing to develop an unshakable confidence in ourselves while cultivating a self-forgetful humility. It is no wonder that we puzzle over how we might proceed. Yet, the tightrope walkers may give us a clue as to how to approach our newly developing discipline. They have to develop skills over a long series of small self-conscious efforts in training, and then, they have to be able to apply those skills in such a way as to be able to perform with confidence. The small daily actions create ingrained patterns so they become effortless and a source of unselfconscious strength.

The concentrated repetition of desirable qualities results in what is called the virtuous circle. The virtues not only become habitual and strong patterns of response but they cultivate in the practitioner a growing sense of self-respect, which can result only from living in harmony with one's highest nature. And when there is a harmony between the interior Self and the lesser self of the earthly personality, the resultant sense of well-being and confidence creates understanding and motivation to strengthen the virtuous responses. Once begun, this virtuous circle brings certain growth along the spiritual path.

The fuel that jumpstarts the practice of spiritually desirable qualities into this virtuous circle is a genuine concern for others and an unassuming practice of the virtues for their own sake—without concern for praise or blame from others. In fact, the resulting self-confidence has nothing to do with judgment by anyone in the outer world, but rather by the inner knowledge of one's inherent value as a spiritual being—the birthright of every human being. Yet our complex emotional/intellectual psyches continually try to draw our attention to ourselves and with that flicker of lost focus, we stumble.

In a March 28, 2008 Bill Moyers interview, Cory Booker, mayor of Newark, New Jersey, confirmed his recognition of the importance of citizens' confidence in their own self worth as a critical factor in resurrecting the respectability of that city. Booker said, "It is a spiritual crisis of people not believing in the greatness of who we are."

The same principle is expressed in *The Man of La Mancha*, a musical based on Cervantes' story about Don Quixote, a comical figure who sees valor and beauty where it is not visible to most others in the world. In perceiving the prostitute Aldonza as "Lady Dulcinea," he prompts her sense of self-worth and thereby gradually transforms her attitude. By the end of the play, she embraces her newfound self-esteem by claiming the name of Dulcinea. One is left with the hope that she has entered into the aforementioned virtuous circle.

This unassuming confidence in one's inherent value and spiritual potential is a critical element for traveling the Path. In a letter of encouragement to a would-be student healer, the Master Morya writes:

> *So now, you my chela, choose and grasp your own destiny. (You wish to heal the sick, —do so; but remember your success will be measured by your faith—in yourself, more than in us. Lose it for a second, and failure will follow. I will give orders to Morya Junior—Olcott—to teach you the mechanical art.) Have faith in your soul power, and you will have success.* (Letter 51, 2nd series)

Traversing the narrow path is an experience in balancing between self-forgetfulness and self-awareness, confidence and hubris, focused effort and sensitivity to others. This is accomplished moment by moment, day by day, as we strive to live with altruism in our hearts and with our minds attuned to the highest good. Realizing the inevitable failures and foibles that occur in the development of skills, we can have infinite patience with ourselves and others, as long as we keep our sight on the ultimate good of all. So let us explore the power of who we really are and forge ahead with an unflinching confidence that will lead us on to the goal of blessing and serving humanity. The way may be impossibly narrow and vertiginously exposed, but it provides direct feedback as we learn to toe the edge with balance and equanimity.

FROM PEBBLES TO STEPPING STONES

THOSE WHO KNOW ME are aware of my penchant for early morning walks. The fresh air and bracing activity penetrate the morning fuzzy-brain fog like nothing else. On several occasions my heel has gotten quite sore before realizing, "Oh, there is a rock in my shoe!" Then, in order to keep up my pace and circulation, I think, "Can I shake it out without stopping?" Or, if I am almost home, "Should I just continue for a few hundred yards more?"

Why on earth would we decide to keep walking after realizing we have a rock in our shoe, and furthermore, why might it take any time at all to realize that the rock is there? We might ask this question with an air of condescension, thinking that surely we ourselves would have better sense than that. Yet consider this same question from the perspective of how we live our lives.

First of all, most of us live with some pain or anguish that is so familiar that we do not even bring it to our conscious awareness. The daily traffic jams and road rage, irritation with family members, resentment toward whatever life has brought us, feelings of anger or inadequacy—these pebbles may irritate our existence for a number of years before we realize that life can be another way. This is not "just the way it is." We do not have to be trapped in this misery. We are conscious beings with unlimited possibilities for growth and change.

After realizing that something may be wrong and needs to be fixed, we often postpone the stop to make needed changes, but keep going, persisting in the same old ruts. How often do we choose to live with the pain rather than change our way of being? We may even decide to chatter about the pain with our traveling companions while still doing nothing about it. It takes time to seek out those hurtful pebbles and reach a willingness to break our stride. In the subtle reaches of our consciousness, we probably question whether we will ever be able to find that at all. So we travel on, without pause to contemplate.

In my far distant past, I learned in psychology class that kittens raised in a cage with vertical bars were confounded when transferred to one with horizontal bars. It was as if they could not even see the differently aligned obstruction. While I recognize that this is a dreadful image to have remained in my mind all these years, I do see a useful comparison. A cage that becomes extremely familiar can become a part of our accepted landscape and so is no longer a part of our consciousness.

Cultural identity and family traditions into which we were born tend to seem like the only normal and "right" approach to life. Behaviors and attitudes pass down from one generation to the next like an immutable script. Even when we rebel against them, they still form the standards by which we measure life. These patterns, which are built into our psyche from birth, are like a pair of sunglasses before our eyes. Colors, clarity, and the amount of light can be drastically affected. It is not until they are removed that one is struck by the impact they had on the perception of the surrounding scene.

Whether we see these patterns in terms of a pebble, a cage, or dark glasses, the nature of consciousness is to accept them as reality. That is why it is said that we live in *maya*, the great illusion. Things are not as they seem, but are distorted by years and lifetimes of conditioning. There is a reality to our existence, but it is not as restrictive as we perceive it to be. If we could only turn an about-face within our minds, the whole spectrum of life would appear differently.

The Buddha said that life is suffering, that by its very nature we will all experience anguish and hardships. But he also said the pain is caused by us, by our attitude of clinging to our conditioning and our desires. We want permanency, stability, power, wealth, comfort, respect, appreciation, and all those good things that attract us. The Buddha called this *attachment*. He said that there is a way out of this dilemma and went on to prescribe the Noble Eightfold Path as the method of deliverance. The Eightfold Path can be summarized as right thought, right motivation, right speech, right action, right livelihood, right effort, right mindfulness, and right concentration.

From this teaching, we can surmise that the removing the pebble is not all that simple. One could take a lifetime to understand and practice any one of these mandates. However, if we do not begin to address the problem, we will never even hope to succeed. Consider beginning with the first step—that of practicing right thought. If we could begin to control these wayward thoughts, to observe them, cultivate the beneficial ones, and begin to recognize ourselves as spiritual beings, the rest would follow. In the Bhagavad Gita, Krishna tells Arjuna that the mind is as difficult to tame as the wind, but that with persistent effort the goal can be achieved. By turning our consciousness in on itself, a gradual shift occurs, one that is almost imperceptible at first. Yet a consistent watchfulness of our thoughts and motives launches a momentum toward awareness. With this turning of our thoughts, we can be assured that the rest will follow. This is what the Greeks called *metanoia*, a complete turning around or reorientation. This word, which appears often in the New Testament, is usually translated "repentance," and Jesus said it was necessary in order to be born again.

The turning around is not just turning the same old processes in a different direction, but rather it is an inside-out reorientation. Instead of directing our thoughts and energy to the level of our outer personality, something convinces us of an inner reality—the true nature of our inner self, connected with all other selves as a part of a greater whole. If we can see life from this perspective, the light of pure spirit will drive away those fuzzy-brain blues.

The painful pebbles of this world will finally penetrate our awareness. Their presence is a gift that finally directs our attention to the importance of addressing the issue. They draw us toward discovery of the problem, and in that discovery lies the opportunity to change. When given proper attention, those pebbles can become our stepping-stones.

> None of you has ever thought of watching, studying and thus profiting by the lessons contained therein, the web of life woven round each of you, yet it is that intangible, yet ever plainly web (to those who would see its working) in that ever open book, sacred in the mystic light around you, that you *could* learn, aye, even those possessed of no clairvoyant powers.
>
> It is the first rule in the daily life of a student of Occultism never to take off his attention from the smallest circumstances that may happen in his own or other fellow-students' lives. ("A Valuable Lesson," *The Theosophist*, September 1954.)

SENSITIVE DEPENDENCE

ALTHOUGH EINSTEIN IS famous for his opinion that "God does not play dice," subsequent scientists have successfully delved into the amazingly unpredictable world of subatomic theory. Light behaves as waves or particles, depending on how the observer measures it; particles appear and disappear seemingly at random, with only a probability of being present at a particular place and time; and chaos theory recognizes the panorama of ever-unfolding patterns produced by irresolvable nonlinear equations.

In this world of the infinite, where it seems that nothing can be nailed down as absolute, we encounter an amazingly important principle: sensitive dependence upon initial conditions. This means that an infinitesimal difference somewhere earlier in an equation will make a major change in the outcome. Rather than "garbage in, garbage out," it is more that one tiny bit of garbage in can result in a mountain of garbage out. One minute modification to ocean temperatures can cause the difference between a destructive storm and a cooling breeze halfway around the world.

Most people who are on the Internet have received the e-mail about plastic bag pollution that has been circulating during the last year. Pictures that graphically illustrate the horrific impact of the mounting accumulation of plastic bags accompany the text cataloging the environmental damage and unnecessary suffering

142

caused to wildlife through this human excess. As the light of awareness dawns on this problem, people all around our nation are beginning to be more careful about the use and disposal of this nonbiodegradable material. In recognition of our power to ameliorate the difficulty, the Theosophical Order of Service has begun promoting reusable shopping bags to replace the offensive plastic. Just as each one of us has contributed to this problem, one bag at a time, so does the solution lie within our power, one bag at a time.

Life is a whole of which each of us is a small but essential part. Up to a certain point, life unfolds without any help from us, but we are the outer edge of life's manifestation, the edge of creativity and dynamic change. The culmination or end point toward which all life moves requires us to cooperate with the high beings that spring forth from within manifestation itself. The parent universe requires the cooperative maturity of its progeny in order to reach its full potential, proving the axiom that creation unfolds from within outward. As the universe progresses in its evolution, its own products are destined in time to develop to the level of becoming cocreators. Creation unfolds according to the spiritual impulse inherent in its own nature—implanted as a spark of the divine omnipresent first principle. Thus the ingenuity and self-responsibility of humankind, for whatever unfathomable reason, are part and parcel of the divine plan and are necessary for it to flower in fullness.

H. P. Blavatsky spoke about our personal responsibility for the well-being and development of this creation. Everything we touch is affected by us, by the quality of our actions, thoughts, and emotions. In volume 12 of the *Collected Works*, she says:

> The earnest Occultist and Theosophist . . . sees and recognizes psychic and spiritual mysteries and profound secrets of nature in every flying particle

of dust, as much as in the giant manifestations of human nature (p. 115).

She also writes:

> Indeed, every organ in our body *has its own memory.* For if it is endowed with a consciousness "of its own kind," every cell must of necessity have also a memory of its own kind, as likewise its own *psychic* and *noëtic* action. Responding to the touch of both a physical and a *metaphysical* Force, the impulse given by the *psychic* (or psycho-molecular) Force will act from *without within;* while that of the *noëtic* (shall we call it Spiritual-dynamical?) Force works *from within without* (p. 368).

In other words, the deepest mysteries of the life force reside within every particle of dust, each particle being influenced by psychic force just as human nature is influenced by the energies it encounters. Every molecule, every cell, has its own consciousness which responds to "spiritual-dynamical" energy. We transmit this energy in our every thought and action, so that every cell or particle we touch is impacted by our vibrations. Our inbreathing and outbreathing draw matter inward, with the potential of transforming, upgrading, and scattering it to repopulate the earth with a finer grade of material. In this way, we are at the frontiers of evolution.

In seeing this process, we begin to realize the profound importance not only of our responsible actions in relation to the physical world, but also of the purity and kindness of our thoughts in relation to the evolutionary progress of manifestation as a whole. If this understanding could truly penetrate our consciousness, we

144

would all put aside the pettiness that arises in our self-seeking human machinations and open our hearts to the whole of humanity. This cannot be accomplished in the abstract, but by dissolving one selfish thought at a time in our true work toward unity and brotherhood with all.

As parts of our nation, we can raise our voices in support of diplomacy, sustainability, and responsible peace, which are so essential for our survival. In our homes we can monitor our thoughts and responses to make them more harmonious and loving, which is so essential for the nurture of our spirits. And in the Theosophical Society we can put aside divisions to focus on building a spiritual unity, which is so absolutely essential for the Society's effectiveness and indeed for its continued existence. Each letting go of old agendas, each reaching out in brotherhood, each stretching beyond self for the greater good—every one of these selfless expressions is a small initial circumstance that can manifest in hugely impactful ways—perhaps far beyond our little imaginings. We are the element for transformation, one thought or action at a time. We have to become the change that we long for—the change that cannot occur unless we do our part—now.

THE STORY TO TELL

I LOVE A good story. As the images of exotic scenery, exciting adventure, tender love, and inspirational insight parade before my inner imagination, I am carried along with them. I thrill or despair, thirst or feel fulfilled as the story unfolds. The trials of the hero become my trials, and the insights become my insights. The alternative reality imprints on my mind as if the event had taken place in the world of my own daily life.

This function of mind was brought home to me during the news releases of the quick thinking and heroism of Captain Chesley B. "Sully" Sullenberger, the pilot of US Airways flight 1549, which in a near disaster collided with a flock of geese during a routine take-off from LaGuardia Airport in New York City on January 15, 2009. With both engines completely blocked, the descending airplane threatened both the lives of the passengers and the residents of the surrounding neighborhoods, which were heavily populated. More people could have lost their lives than in the World Trade Center disaster. Yet by the time it was made public, all passengers were safely accounted for and the aircraft was floating down the Hudson River, having done no serious injury to people or property.

News stories generally inundate our minds with violence, corruption, greed, and disaster so that we can become supersaturated with negativity. Cynicism and pessimism seem to be signs of being well-informed and sophisticated. For some reason, the public in general thrives on the sensational, the scandalous. And we get caught up in that mentality, swept along on a wave of fear and outrage.

This story had the opposite effect. As the story unfolded of the miraculous landing and rescue of 150 passengers and five crew members, I was filled with tears of joy and gratitude. Immediately after the crash landing, ferries and other boats redirected their courses to the site in order to bring all safely to shore. The serendipitous choices, quick thinking, and heroic efforts of all involved created a drama of what seemed to be a cooperation of divine and human forces in order to bring about a miracle. It was as if I had been there and I had been saved, and I was filled with gratitude.

Each of us has this capacity of imagination, which is a manifestation of the universal creative principle that imbues us with self-consciousness and self-reflection. This is the quality of humanness that places us above the animal stage, although a little lower than the angels. We are an embodiment of the creative principle. The way we process our experiences, memories, and reactions creates a unique environment for each of us. Each sees the world differently through a particular mind-set. This mind-set creates our world of challenges for this lifetime. *Kama-manas*, or the mental-emotional functions, are the very trap of *maya*, the illusions whereby we develop patterns of seeing and become ensnared in our own mental constructs.

Our emotional entanglements make us see what we expect to see and suffer what we anticipate. This is not to say that everything is in our minds or that we necessarily choose our suffering. We cannot dismiss the power of suffering by the flippant attitude that "they have brought it upon themselves and just have to deal with it." Things happen that have complex causes and complex solutions. We have to deal with the paradigm in which we are presently caught. It is true that emotional attachment to the vicissitudes of life is the root cause of our suffering, just as the Buddha observed. Yet we have to figure out how to deal with the here and now. Now that we are in this mess, how can we begin to grow and work through it?

We are the prisoners of the accumulation of our thoughts, but we are also the masters of our fate. We can decide what we want to tell ourselves over and over again and thus create beneficial, or at least harmless, scenes that reverberate through our minds. As we read in The Voice of the Silence, "If thou wouldst not be slain by them, then must thou harmless make thy own creations, the children of thy thoughts, unseen, impalpable, that swarm round humankind, the progeny and heirs to man and his terrestrial spoils."

Our minds work in strange and mysterious ways, catching and holding on to whatever we feed them. As writer and actor Benjamin Busch said in an interview on National Public Radio, "Who knows how the folds of the mind work, but things get caught in there." Consciousness is sticky; things get caught in there, usually in unintended ways. Our minds believe and hold on to what they are fed on a daily basis. And the longer we chew on an idea, the tighter it sticks.

It is not easy but we do have the ability to determine the character of our steady diet. The Bhagavad Gita says, "For the mind is verily, restless, O Krishna; it is impetuous, strong and difficult to bend. I deem it as hard to curb as the wind."

Whenever we encounter a story that brings tears of joy to the heart, let us dwell on the miracle of heroic service to others. Just as the airplane rescue sent waves of happy gratitude around our nation, so we can magnify the little unsung deeds of generosity to be found in our ordinary encounters. Whether large or small, the light of consciousness enables these deeds to become more power-ful in transforming ourselves and our world.

Each day, let us look for these moments of joy or self-forgetfulness, forgiveness, loving-kindness, or any quality that lifts the human spirit. Let us look for opportunities to immerse ourselves in books, videos, music, and works of visual art that inspire those qualities. These positive aspects will stick in the folds of our minds and begin the healing process. In this way we begin to become the peace that we all long for. This is the story of the ages that all long to hear. This is the story to tell with our whole being.

FLY A KITE

ONE THOUSAND KITES in the air at the same time! This was the goal of the Wheaton Sesquicentennial Commission when they put out an all-call for kite flyers from the area to gather in one of the local parks last spring. They were hoping to set a world's record for the most kites flying at once. The winds didn't cooperate, but it was a festive gathering drawing kiters of all sorts together for the grand attempt. Although the count was a mere 800, the event created a myriad of shapes and colors dotting the skies.

Besides the lack of cooperation from the winds (and we live near Chicago, which is known as the Windy City), one reason the event didn't meet its goal may be that our general culture isn't very savvy about kiting. We can find some kites in the stores, but rarely do we see many in the air. This is probably because there is a real art to kite flying, and what may seem like a simple hobby in fact requires a certain level of skill.

Think about all the parts of a simple kite that have to be in balance. First is the framework, which has to be tough, light, balanced, and flexible. It has to be carefully designed, since it is the structure on which all else hangs. Then the wind-resistant covering that holds it all together adds lift, design, and color. Yet even with these details carefully crafted, the kite cannot get off the ground if it does not have a tail to keep it in balance.

These elements of a kite can be likened to the spiritual life. The structure or framework is composed of the familiar Theosophical triad of study, meditation, and service. These are the supporting spines of our practice, without which any effort will fall flat. The study of the Ageless Wisdom, against which we can measure our experience of nature within and without, provides the strength of understanding that can carry us through the winds of fortune.

The more we know about the universe and its laws, the more we begin to see the necessity of an altruistic spirit. A greater understanding of our own nature creates in us an absolute realization of our unity with all. Without this generous and open-hearted attitude, our spiritual kite will not be structurally sound and will finally collapse under the weight of its own self-preoccupation.

Yet study and service alone lack cohesiveness. They require the strong binder of meditation, which holds these elements together in a meaningful way so that they are firmly anchored in our consciousness. Meditation creates the still insight through which our own individuality can unfold its beautiful design. We are like snowflakes: no two are exactly alike. Meditation reaches deeply within to tune into that interior essence so that each one of us is able to express his or her own distinctive character.

With these foundations well in place, we are on our way, but without the covering to provide the lift, we are still earthbound. That covering can be compared to the essential element of inspiration. Study, meditation, and service can be quite consistent, but until the element of inspiration is introduced, our practice can fall flat. This is a part of the beauty and art of building our soul's kite. The sources of inspiration are myriad and unpredictable. For some, it may be Taizé chanting or singing the Indian devotional songs known as *bhajans*; for some it may be the veneration of Jesus, Buddha, Allah, saints from the past, or present-day teachers; for others it may be ringing bells, lighting candles, or praying in a chapel. The colorful practices of the traditions we hold dear call to the depths of our being, resonating with the intrinsic patterns of our individual natures and drawing us toward the heights. These multifaceted practices, which bring inspiration through beauty and devotion when observed in full consciousness and joined within the framework of study, meditation, and service, create an inner structure that will be sensitive to every breath of wind from universal spirit.

The caution to be sounded here is that we all have to realize that the shape and color of our kites are not the only kinds there are or should be. Besides making this a very boring and regimented world, this would essentially tie our kites down to self-centeredness, pride, and exclusivity. These will never fly!

Finally, the remaining element required for an effective kite is a proper tail to provide balance and steady orientation as the winds blow to and fro. I think we can say that the element that provides this balance is the attempt to live by high ethical standards each and every moment of our daily lives. This consistent development of character steadies our efforts and generates the necessary stability.

All of this we do in preparation, but we never know when the wind will catch us and lift us to the heights. We have to be diligent, trust the wisdom of those who have experience in the flight of spirit, and remain willing to keep trying and learning. If our practice and inspiration are soundly based and our daily lives reflect all that we know, we will be holding our souls aloft in readiness. We will be prepared to catch the smallest breeze.

If we are prepared and ready, the spirit will move us and lift us into the heavens. And if we Theosophists as a group can work together sharing knowledge and helping one another, then we can have an assortment of many-colored kites of consciousness held in readiness so that we can have many more than a thousand spirits joined in heart and breath, dotting the cosmos and shielding humanity.

Build your spiritual kite carefully day by day and hold it ever at ready so that in the twinkling of the universal eye, we will unite as a band of worldwide servers. The many shapes, designs, and colors of our beings united in spirit will offer far more than a spectacle of color or shapes filling the sky: we can be the critical mass to improve, beautify, and, yes, even transform our world.

WHAT ABOUT THE FUTURE?

WHAT IS OUR PURPOSE? What are we, who care deeply about the world, to do? If we are committed to the work of the adepts, the inner founders of the Theosophical Society, how can we stay focused and positive in the face of seemingly endless turmoil and violence? In our younger years of high idealism, we might have felt that we could save the world—and that we would save it. Some young readers of this piece may still feel that way, and I hope they are successful. However, as time goes by and as our world broadens to include the entire globe, the problems can seem insurmountable.

In considering what we might do, we need to first look at where and who we are before ascertaining where we want to go and how to get there. Often when my husband, David, and I are driving some-where and we get turned around (a less objectionable term than "getting lost"), I am assigned to be the map reader. As David cruises by street signs that either glide by too quickly or are too obscured by glare for my eyes to focus on, I am totally lost as to where we are on the map—and am no help whatsoever. We have to first figure out where we are, either by seeing an identifying landmark or by stopping to read a sign. (Real men do not ask directions.) A map or plan requires both a starting and an ending point in order to be useful. I recognize that this analogy may be lost on those of you who have graduated to GPS systems in your cars, but even though the new technology can tell you where you are, you cannot move ahead without knowing the address of your destination.

So let us start with where we are. Have we formed a coherent nucleus of the universal brotherhood of humanity? Are we at least working in that direction? Are we building into our own characters a willingness to listen to our brothers and sisters? Do we consider kindness as a primary motivation for our actions? Of course, as imperfect human beings, we probably cannot answer totally in the affirmative, but to the degree that we can, we can be assured that we are generally headed in the right direction.

We are currently in a time of transition from the old Piscean energies of belief structures and authority figures to the uncharted waters of Aquarius, the age of cooperative knowledge and understanding. The networking capabilities of the Internet personify the spirit of this new age. Although for many of us this heightened fluidity creates stress and confusion, somehow we have to be able to regain our bearings in the cross-currents of these times. Perhaps we can be more hopeful if we realize that the chaos we see without and within is a necessary pathway of transition.

There are many things that we cannot understand or predict, but one thing is certain. If we are to have a life worth living, if we are to travel toward a better future, we must incorporate compassion and tolerance as an essential component of our being. Many of our standard landmarks may be changing, but the mandate toward brotherhood/sisterhood remains constant throughout the ages. Jesus told us to love our neighbors as ourselves. He also taught that we could not love our spiritual parent, whom we have not seen, if we could not love our brothers or sisters, whom we have seen.

So wherever we find ourselves, the one certain direction is to seek to build relationships in which we touch spirit to spirit, in which we are bonded by a mutual understanding of unity and

155

ageless spiritual principles. In the June 2009 issue of *TheoSophia* magazine from New Zealand, President Warwick Keys stated that if a number of people equal to the square root of one percent of the population would meditate on the same thing, it would have far-reaching results. I am not sure of the source of his figures, but I am convinced of the inherent truth of his statement. I propose that this same kind of disproportionate outcome exists relative to our impact on the world.

We always have the option of following some of the divisive patterns of the past, when members of our band stood divided against one another. Many times our Society has had disagreements and splits over issues that could have been resolved if egos and personalities could have been put aside. Our penchant for fractiousness can be reviewed in the historical family tree of American Theosophy by Dorothy Bell on page 22 of this issue. This history highlights the need for us to increase and strengthen our bonds of fellowship as Theosophists—in our lodges, in our federations, at the national and international levels—wherever and however we can be drawn together in ways that make those bonds possible. Only by working together can we transform the world.

Once forged, those bonds become living strands within our nucleus and form what Buddhists call our sangha, our spiritual family, which provides spiritual support and encouragement. This kind of spiritual family used to be more or less limited to one's physical location, but can now be extended worldwide. As a part of the new wave of possibilities brought to us by our modern culture, our territory is the entire planet. The masters surely understood this when they inspired the impulse toward forming the Society, as did the French scientist and philosopher Pierre Teilhard de Chardin when he postulated the concept of the noosphere—a dimension of consciousness that encompasses the globe. In both instances, they saw a spiritual network as being a goal of humanity as well as the ultimate salvation of our world. Grasping this idea alone can turn the tide away from violence and the clash of civilizations.

Theosophical author Geoffrey Hodson glimpsed the reality of this inner fellowship as spanning not only national borders but also the demarcations of time. In chapter 7 of *Thus Have I Heard* he wrote:

> Nature has placed many of us in incarnation in the West. We are being borne upon the crest of a wave of materialism and of intense physical activity. We must learn to achieve and to maintain that spiritual poise and inner realisation which was ours in olden days. We no longer enjoy the close physical companionships of long ago, when we prayed and worked together in the temples, monasteries and mystery schools, for we are now spread all over the world. The old association remains but it is now mental. We are united by our common acceptance of the teachings of the Ancient Wisdom. No matter in what part of the world we may be, we are in reality one body corporate. Our ancient friendships and relationships show themselves today as we draw together in the same great cause, and follow the same glorious Leaders, who are the Masters of the Wisdom, and Their exalted representatives in the outer world.

In this sense we are to be the cornerstone of the future religions of humanity. Our activities and studies have to draw us toward this kind of bonding or they become exercises in futility. How this translates into specific programs we can only work at day by day, but this much I know: the means has to be inherent in the end sought. In other words, our goal is present at every crossroads: every step along the way has to include elements of the goal. If this goal is an unfolding of universal brotherhood/sisterhood, then the map calls for each one of us to incorporate that into the patterns of our work in daily life and for the Society. Each such spiritual bond is a treasure, a gift not only to ourselves but also to the stability of today's world and to the vast future stretching before us.

APPLIED SCIENCE

IN 2002 AT fourteen years of age, William Kamkwamba could not return to school because of extended drought and impoverishment in his small village in Malawi, Africa. Discouraged but not defeated, this entrepreneurial boy continued his education in the local library whenever his chores permitted. Some spark of hope prompted him to dream about using ideas he read about to solve problems for his family and village. He began collecting scrap plastic, bicycle and machinery parts, and scouring the dump for all sorts of odd pieces of junk.

As the villagers scoffed, his contraption grew into a sixteen-foot high curiosity—which he called his "juju" or magic. Ridicule turned to amazement when he was able to power a light bulb from the power generated by his improvised windmill. From this humble beginning, his project grew to power all the needs for his family's meager household and to pump precious water for his and other families' needs. Following the law of attraction, the more successful he was with his project, the more visitors and benefactors contributed to help his efforts. Now at twenty-three, Mr. Kamkwamba has collaborated with journalist Bryan Mealer for the 2009 publication of his story, titled *The Boy Who Harnessed the Wind*, and has traveled extensively for speaking engagements. He is continuing his education through a number of unique opportunities.

What began as a defeat was transformed into a heartwarming success story not because of outside help, but because this young man determined to make use of all the knowledge and opportunities he had at hand. He opened his eyes and saw the possibilities, and then committed all of his energies to developing the possibilities into realities. There was nothing earthshakingly new about what he did, but for him it was a major accomplishment. He absorbed all the knowledge at his disposal, internalized it, and acted on it in order to address his problems.

This is one of the reasons we are so fascinated with science. It provides a way of looking at our world as it is in order to understand it more fully, and by understanding to see windows of opportunity more clearly. However, factual knowledge by itself is no more than a temporary relief for an obscure mental itch unless it is transformed into usefulness through analysis, synthesis, or analogy. Without some application it will just be buried in the seas of time. We are responsible to make the best use of whatever knowledge we have available to us. It is not sufficient just to let information pass through our brains, unused, on the way to the oblivion of uselessness.

Consider how little funding is currently available to explore ways to treat chicken pox now that the vaccine has all but eliminated it—or to develop better iron lungs for polio victims—or to develop quieter typewriters now that they have been displaced by computers. Although these developments were important at the time, once their usefulness is over, they fall by the wayside. On the whole, funding for research and development follow the threads of applicability. We want to understand so that we have better control. Science is valued because it delivers facts that can make a difference in feeding the hungry, curing ills, or inspiring the dreams of possibilities in young minds.

Because in a world of measurable things, people will believe and abide by measurable things—even to the degree of hand washing and use of seatbelts. If statistics or research indicates the efficacy of a practice, we will tend to abide by those findings. Otherwise we are not convinced, nor do we change our behavior. Perhaps this is part of the reasoning behind KH's statement, "Modern science is our best ally" (*Mahatma Letters*, no. 65). Most of us want tangible proof. Science can convince us of deep spiritual truths if nothing else can.

Since the time that statement was written, KH's statements "that we recognize but one element in *Nature (whether spiritual or physical) outside which there can be no Nature since it is Nature itself* . . . and that consequently spirit and matter are one" (ibid.) have been vindicated time and again. He was saying that unity and interrelatedness permeate the universe and that universe is an interrelated whole of "spirit-matter" at every level of existence. Although such ideas seemed an impossibility at the time, through science we have come to accept that energy and matter are convertible, the consciousness or spirit of an observer influences the physical outcome of an experiment, and action on one atom can affect another, no matter the distance between them. Every day science confirms the seamless nature of our universe, and realizing this she convinces us of this reality.

These insights are not idle fancies to tickle our intellect. They have implications that translate to the personal responsibility of each one of us to recognize our innate unity with all, and in doing so we have the basis for applying altruism to every aspect of our lives. This knowledge of the unitive nature of the universe should convince us to apply these principles in active altruism. If we are so connected in every fiber of our being, then whatever we do or think impacts all others, since in the deepest sense they are not separate from us.

As Madame Blavatsky wrote in *The Key to Theosophy* (section 4):

> The one self has to forget itself for the many selves. Let me answer you in the words of a true Philale- theian, an F. T. S., who has beautifully expressed it in the *Theosophist:* "What every man needs first is to find himself, and then take an honest inventory of his subjective possessions, and, bad or bankrupt as it may be, it is not beyond redemption if we set about it in earnest." But how many do? All are willing to work for their own development and progress; very few for those of others. To quote the same writer again: "Men have been deceived and deluded long enough; they must break their idols, put away their shams, and go to work for themselves—nay, there is one little word too much or too many, for he who works for himself had better not work at all; rather let him work himself for others, for all. For every flower of love and char- ity he plants in his neighbour's garden, a loathsome weed will disappear from his own, and so this garden of the gods—Humanity—shall blossom as a rose."

Let us be like the young man who took advantage of every piece of information available to him and apply that practice to our life issues. If something is missing in our spiritual life, if life seems meaningless, or if we simply wonder what it is all about, then perhaps the elixir resides in putting into practice those things we already know. If we accept the scientific reality of wholeness, of our intrinsic relationship with all others, then we need to begin applying the resultant implications. If unity is a universal law, then brotherhood/sisterhood is its logical application.

Take the parts and pieces of understanding we find in our minds and hearts and use their full range of possibilities. Begin the process of building altruism into every thought and action—even if it seems out of step with the rest of our culture. Our mandate as Theosophists is altruism. Through its practice we will be able to harness untold power for the benefit of all, one flower of love and charity at a time.

THE CHARTER OF COMPASSION

THE COLLISIONS AND clashes of cultures and belief systems have reached epic proportions. The problem partly stems from the attitude of Christian colonialists over the last 500 years, who were so convinced that theirs was the only way that they felt totally justified in subjugating the "heathen" races. In fact they used what has come to be known as the Doctrine of Discovery to validate their territorial claims all over the world. This doctrine traces its origins to a series of pronouncements by fifteenth-century popes that non-Christian lands could be "discovered" and subdued; the original inhabitants were classified as occupants without any sovereign rights to their land. Using this idea as justification, the colonialists destroyed millions of indigenous people and their cultures. This attitude has slid to the background in recent decades, but it still colors the attitudes of many people, influencing political policies and causing immense psychological harm to the point where it has boiled to overflowing in the violent events of today.

At its founding in 1875, the Theosophical Society was the first organized effort to develop appreciation for faiths beyond that of the dominant culture. The founders of the Theosophical Society, especially those inner guides—the adepts—recognized the urgent need for humankind to learn to live together and to honor one another as brothers and sisters of the spirit—all one family inter-dependent and partaking of one substance, one nature, and one destiny. Again and again they emphasized the importance of our First Object: "To form a nucleus of the universal brotherhood of humanity regardless of race, creed, sex, caste, or color." Their work for the formation of a strong nucleus of a compassionate brother-hood for all people was aimed at permeating and changing the culture of oppression before it was too late. This was probably the main reason that they even agreed to become as publicly visible as the forming of the Society required. The currents of conflict and violence were in motion, and they needed to do whatever possi-ble to stem the tide.

By 1893, although some in the Western world were waking up to the presence of other faiths, Christian culture still prevailed, as exemplified by the first World's Parliament of Religions, which was held in Chicago that year. Its organizers basically viewed religions other than Christianity merely as interesting oddities, so they were quite amazed at the results. They were stunned by the popularity of the Hindu teacher Swami Vivekananda and of Annie Besant's famous oration. Reflecting a gradual shift in attitude, the second such event, held a hundred years later in 1993, was renamed the Parliament of the World's Religions in order to acknowledge that each religion has its own validity.

However, as we now so sadly recognize, humanity has not been quick enough in changing its attitudes. We have been entrenched in habitual thought and unwieldy institutions; finally the pain of abuse and disenfranchisement exploded into our consciousness with the terrorist attacks of September 11, 2001. Now we know that inter-faith understanding is not just a nice thing to do, but is essential for the welfare and survival of all people. All over the planet differ-ent sects are attacking each other. No one is immune—Christians,

Muslims, Buddhists, Hindus, Jews, and others are all the brunt of someone else's hatred.

As a continuation of the efforts to build interreligious understanding, a number of subsequent Parliament events have been held, the most recent being the Parliament for the World's Religions that David and I attended in Melbourne, Australia, in December 2009. Thousands of thinkers and religious leaders gathered to dialogue, honor the universal search for spiritual meaning, recognize the plight of indigenous people, and promote environmental sustainability as an inherent responsibility for the well-being of all. Foremost in the presenters' and participants' minds were ways to heal the rift between peoples and between people and their environment, all within the context of their religious traditions.

Notable among the presentations was the Charter of Compassion, which had been prepared by the well-known religious author Karen Armstrong in consultation with a number of Jewish, Christian, and Muslim leaders. Signatories of note include His Holiness the Dalai Lama, Archbishop Desmond Tutu, and former United Nations Human Rights High Commissioner Mary Robinson. The charter calls for the establishment of an alliance of individuals, organizations, and communities to advocate for global change. It calls for a complete change of attitude with a renewed sensitivity to all.

I urge each one who reads this piece to copy the Charter of Compassion given below and post it on your wall as a daily reminder of this global ethic of sensitivity. And I further ask that you consider promoting it in your groups, among friends, and in your spiritual communities. In doing so, we will be joining thousands of others who have been touched by this message, and little by little we can turn the tide of intolerance and move toward the Theosophical ideal of the universal brotherhood of humanity.

CHARTER FOR COMPASSION

The principle of compassion lies at the heart of all religious, ethical, and spiritual traditions, calling us always to treat all others as we wish to be treated ourselves. Compassion impels us to work tirelessly to alleviate the suffering of our fellow creatures, to dethrone ourselves from the center of our world and put another there, and to honor the inviolable sanctity of every single human being, treating everybody, without exception, with absolute justice, equity, and respect.

It is also necessary in both public and private life to refrain consistently and empathically from inflicting pain. To act or speak violently out of spite, chauvinism, or self-interest, to impoverish, exploit, or deny basic rights to anybody, and to incite hatred by denigrating others—even our enemies—is a denial of our common humanity. We acknowledge that we have failed to live compassionately and that some have even increased the sum of human misery in the name of religion.

We therefore call upon all men and women
— To restore compassion to the center of morality and religion;
— To return to the ancient principle that any interpretation of scripture that breeds violence, hatred, or disdain is illegitimate;
— To ensure that youth are given accurate and respectful information about other traditions, religions, and cultures;

— To encourage a positive appreciation of cultural
and religious diversity;
— To cultivate an informed empathy with the suffering of all human beings, even those regarded as
enemies.

We urgently need to make compassion a clear, luminous, and dynamic force in our polarized world.
Rooted in a principled determination to transcend
selfishness, compassion can break down political,
dogmatic, ideological, and religious boundaries. Born
of our deep interdependence, compassion is essential
to human relationships and to a fulfilled humanity.
It is the path to enlightenment and indispensable to
the creation of a just economy and peaceful global
community.

KEEP YOUR EYES ON THE PRIZE

CAN YOU REMEMBER learning how to ride a bike? After one has learned, it seems so natural that the actual learning is quickly forgotten—except by the traumatized parents who were trying to help the process. "It is all about balance," they would say encouragingly. So it proceeded through trial and error, until pretty soon the catastrophic wobble transformed into a tentatively directed ride before bursting into an exhilarating junket at full speed ahead. The balance was not something to be told or read about, but to do. Once mastered, the skill is always accessible; it may become rusty with disuse, but can quickly be recaptured.

Yet, balance has other, more subtle components. Focused attention is required to avoid the ordinary small obstacles such as a stone or bump in the road or a change in pavement, but attention must also be directed toward a wider outlook. If one kept eyes down on each little obstacle a tumble would surely result, or one might suddenly find oneself wrapped around a telephone pole.

Quite obviously this applies to our lives in general and particularly to the life of an aspirant. There are many levels of balanced functioning to be achieved, each building on the former and each requiring practice and attention. At each point in our growth, what we have already learned seems simple and what still lies ahead seems daunting. However the three principles of balance, focus, and a constant eye to the horizon are essential elements of our practice. I recently ran across several little aphorisms by George S. Arundale (GSA), president of the international TS from 1934 to 1945, written in 1919 in a little book titled *The Way of Service*. I will use them to highlight the three principles mentioned above.

Balance: "Do not allow the force of your affection for another to disturb either your balance or his" GSA writes. "Your service must strengthen and not weaken." Isn't it interesting that at the very outset we have to learn to balance what we generally call love? A multitude of sins can parade under the guise of love, such as an attachment to our way of defining a person and how they must act. In our desire to be helpful we need to keep balanced within boundaries so that each has the space to unfurl his or her own unique potential.

Balance in human relationships requires a great deal of self-awareness. We see through the filters of self-interest and protection of the group we belong to—whatever that may be. Each layer of learning about ourselves reveals one more way in which we might fool ourselves into thinking that our motives are purely altruistic when they actually may be quite self serving. And moving beyond self-interest to protecting our cultural bias with which we identify, we can become quite irrational in the way we react to and value our brothers and sisters. This has manifested in many ways including women's issues, homophobia, race relations, and religious intolerance. All these throw us totally off balance in our view of reality.

Focus: "Do not be jealous of another's greater power of service," urges GSA, "rather be glad that a greater power exists to help those whom your own weaker force may be unable to reach." In other words, recognize the ideal of benefiting humankind as the goal rather than whether you might shine or be recognized for any great talent. There are very few truly great people in the world and it is a certain bet that a part of their repertoire is humility. Even so, humanity has such a wide array of talents that excelling in one area is usually balanced by some other weakness. Comparing ourselves to others is like concentrating on the little pebbles in the road, assuring a certain crash.

We have been told by many religious teachings not to worry about the glamour of admiration or praise. Jesus told his disciples to pray in private rather than in public where everyone would recognize one for their righteousness. Krishnamurti penned in the little book *At the Feet of the Master* that your mind "wishes itself to feel proudly separate" and calculates on behalf of self instead of helping others. Beware: anything that feeds the ravenous wolf of self is sure to result in the inevitable crash. As the saying goes, "Pride goes before the fall and mighty pride goes before a mighty fall."

A constant eye: "The less a person thinks about himself, says GSA, "the more he is really paying attention to his growth. Each little act of service returns to the doer in the shape of an added power to serve." To keep "a constant eye toward the ideal of human progression and perfection which the secret science depicts" as HPB stated in the Golden Stairs, our goal is to lift our eyes beyond our personal self to the good of the whole. This kind of habitual view is developed only through the practice of returning our gaze to the horizon again and again, whenever we begin feeling a bit off-balance. With the eyes of our soul uplifted toward this wide view, we gain a powerful tool for holding steady in our travels through life. Our great prize, if we keep our balance, focus, and vision, is the "reward past all telling—the power to bless and save humanity."

There *is* a road, steep and thorny, beset with perils of every kind, but yet a road, and it leads to the very heart of the Universe: I can tell you how to find those who will show you the secret gateway that opens inward only, and closes fast behind the neophyte for evermore. There is no danger that dauntless courage cannot conquer; there is no trial that spotless purity cannot pass through; there is no difficulty that strong intellect cannot surmount. For those who win onwards there is reward past all telling—the power to bless and save humanity; for those who fail, there are other lives in which success may come. (H. P. Blavatsky, *Collected Works*, 13:219)

THE TRUTH

I AM DRAWN to the simplicity and beauty of the motto of the Theosophical Society: *There is no religion higher than Truth.* What is truth? Does it change? Is it absolute? Is it relative? In our lives we often have to determine the truth of a situation. Are we seeing all sides clearly? In the midst of our own personal prejudices, propaganda from friend and foe, and our inherent need to be "right," it is most difficult to determine what is actually true. We might be able to string together certain facts, but do they reveal the truth?

We use accumulated facts to develop our sense of purpose in life—our sense of what is really true and meaningful. But truth keeps moving and growing. Is a two-year-old wrong to think that its mother's primary function in life is to see that all its needs are met? What about the same person at age seven, or ten, or fifteen? How about at ages twenty-one, thirty-one, or fifty-one? At some point a supposedly unchanging truth becomes totally erroneous.

This may seem to be a simplistic example, but it points to an important principle. The set of ideas that we consider to be true creates our worldview, our sense of all existence and its purposes. Human beings seem to be the only creatures on earth that demand to find meaning in existence. A part of our makeup as a soul on its "obligatory pilgrimage," as the third fundamental proposition in *the Secret Doctrine* tells us, is to acquire individuality, and then to grow beyond that individuality, "first by natural impulse, and then by self-induced and self-devised efforts . . . through personal effort and merit throughout a long series of metempsychoses and reincarnations." The search for understanding, meaning, and truth is a part of our very nature. We cannot get away from it. We are endowed with a discerning consciousness that seeks to understand.

Yet paradoxically, this very structure of consciousness tends to keep us from getting at the truth. Consciousness becomes set in its own patterns, developed through long ages of evolution and influenced by every experience of this lifetime. Once we start thinking along a certain track, we set grooves of thinking that reinforce themselves. We are not as free as we like to think, because our consciousness sees reflections of itself wherever it looks. Some have described aspects of these grooves or patterns as our paradigms—the set of assumptions through which we filter all information.

A good example of an outworn and blinding paradigm can be seen in the Swiss watchmaking industry. In the 1960s Swiss inventors were the first to develop the concept of a quartz timepiece, but it was not accepted there. The craftsmen viewed this innovation with disdain, considering it inferior to the long-respected skill of making watches with finely intermeshed gears and gems. Their paradigm didn't allow for a totally different mechanism. And so the idea was perfected by the Japanese, who sold the first commercial quartz movement timepieces by Seiko. Soon thereafter American entrepreneurs developed and began marketing inexpensive quartz watches; particularly notable was the flood of cheap Timex watches on the market. Now there is little call for the fine skills of crafting small, gear-driven timepieces, and a whole industry has long since collapsed and had to reinvent itself.

Another example is the extensive use of stenographers in the last century. What seemed to be a stable profession was quickly made obsolete, first by dictating machines and then by the rapid expansion of computer technology. Today even executives manage much of their own correspondence through e-mail, and recently even through the ever-improving voice recognition software that is now available. The realities of our world and culture are constantly in flux—particularly in this age of technological advances.

Although we need to be able to develop flexible thinking, our thought patterns are so deeply ingrained that that they are present even at the cellular level. Writing in *Theosophy in Australia* (September 2009), Edi Bilimoria recently cited an amazing example from Paul Pearsall's book *The Heart's Code*. Shortly after receiving a heart transplant from a ten-year-old girl who had been murdered, the eight-year-old recipient began having recurring nightmares about the man who had murdered her donor. She was sure that she could identify the murderer. According to the documentation, "the time, the weapon, the place, the clothes he wore, what the little girl he killed had said to him . . . everything the little heart transplant recipient reported was completely accurate," and led to the killer's arrest.

As Theosophists, we are not surprised to realize that memories are recorded even in the physical body. The idea that the emotional and mental fields are permeated by thought forms and habitual thinking is central to the Theosophical understanding of the human makeup. These memories and patterns of thought are ever with us, coloring all that we know of life. Our memories and repeated thoughts about them are the building blocks of our patterns of consciousness, our *vrittis* as they are called in Sanskrit. These patterns or *vrittis* are such an important inhibitor to seeing clearly that in the *Yoga Sutras*, Patanjali tells us that the essential purpose of yoga is their cessation—and thus the stilling or clearing of the mind. To begin to rid ourselves of these restrictive patterns is to begin to open our consciousness to the perception of truth.

H. P. Blavatsky outlined some of the steps required for this clearing in her text "The Golden Stairs." The steps include a clean life, an open mind, a pure heart, an eager intellect, and a readiness to give and receive advice and instruction. She referred to these qualities as some of the "golden stairs up the steps of which the learner may climb to the temple of divine wisdom."

Vincent de Paul, a French Catholic priest of the seventeenth century who was later canonized, was deeply concerned about the search for truth in the lives of his monastics and congregants. He urged them to practice discernment using a three-step method. The first requirement was to have an unrestricted readiness. This could be defined as an unprejudiced open mind, with a willingness to see beyond any personal agenda. Then with this clear mind, one is to carefully weigh the evidence and to seek counsel from sources one deems wise. I would add to that a large dash of common sense— the sense within us that can perceive the clear ring of truth.

What then might serve as a measuring stick by which to test the efficacy of common sense? The only way to reduce the blinding effects of our personal prejudices is to move away from our focus on self. This is the way to develop unrestricted readiness, a willingness to drop old patterns, an openness to unfolding truth. The test of the truth of an idea is to consider what kind of person it makes you. If it is a mature view aligned with truth, it will be one that diminishes your sense of self-importance.

Master Koot Hoomi spoke to this point in an 1884 letter addressing problems that were occurring in the Theosophical lodges in Europe:

You do not find certain recent letters and notes of mine—including the one to the treasurer of the L[ondon] L[odge], "philosophical" and in my usual style. It could scarcely be helped: I wrote but on the business of the moment—as I am doing now— and had no time for philosophy. With the L. L. and most of the other Western Branches of the T. S. in a deplorable state, philosophy may be invoked to restrain one's impatience, but the chief thing called for at present, is some practicable scheme for dealing with the situation. Some, most unjustly, try to make H[enry] S[teel] O[lcott] and H. P. B., solely responsible for the state of things. Those two are, say, far from perfect—in some respects, quite the opposite. But they have that in them (pardon the eternal repetition but it is being as constantly overlooked) which we have but too rarely found elsewhere — UNSELFISHNESS, and an eager readiness for self-sacrifice for the good of others; what a "multitude of sins" does not this cover! It is but a truism, yet I say it, that in adversity alone can we discover the real man. It is a true manhood when one boldly accepts one's share of the collective Karma of the group one works with, and does not permit oneself to be embittered, and to see others in blacker colours than reality, or to throw all blame upon some one "black sheep," a victim, specially selected. Such a true man as that we will ever protect and, despite his shortcomings, assist to develop the good he has in him. Such an one is sublimely *unselfish*; he sinks his personality in his cause, and takes no heed of discomforts or personal obloquy unjustly fastened upon him (*The Mahatma Letters*, chronological edition, no. 131).

Now here is something that we can learn from the spotty history of our beginnings: to move forward for the purposes of our founders and their teachers, we must look first to ourselves—each one of us. Are we approaching all aspects of Theosophical work with "UNSELFISHNESS, and an eager readiness for self-sacrifice for the good of others"? Do we avoid bitterness and fault-finding as we work onward for the higher cause? Are we more concerned about the good of the whole than about being right? Can we ignore unjust criticisms and backbiting and return gentleness and compassion? If each one of us can measure up to this high standard given in *The Mahatma Letters*, then we will be protected in spite of our shortcomings. And we will always be assisted in developing the good in ourselves and in our beloved Society. If we can carry this truth with us in all that we do for the Society, it will live as a flaming beacon for all humanity well into the future!

ARE WE HAVING FUN YET?

OUR TRUE SELF is a journeying pilgrim, experiencing many adventures and misadventures in order to learn and grow. These experiences are not generally what our personality would choose, but are tests, trials, puzzles to solve, or opportunities to develop skillful actions and useful service. They bring us to the creative moment of crisis which elicits growth from within.

As *The Secret Doctrine* says, the progressive journey of a soul is one of the basic principles of our cosmos. The esoteric tradition teaches "the fundamental identity of all Souls with the Universal Over-Soul, the latter being itself an aspect of the Unknown Root; and the obligatory pilgrimage for every Soul—a spark of the former—through the Cycle of Incarnation (or 'Necessity') in accordance with Cyclic and Karmic law, during the whole term." (This quotation and the others in this article are from the proem of *The Secret Doctrine*, I, 17.)

The recent and wildly popular movie *Avatar* portrays the situation of a soul essence inhabiting a body and even moving from one body to another. Although in the story advanced technology is used to achieve this purpose, the symbolism is fascinating. The soul essence of the hero, a paraplegic Marine in this world, is able to inhabit and energize an alien form on an alien planet. As a newcomer to a strangely different body, he has to adapt to his

179

new physical form, learn the mores of the surrounding culture, and develop some mastery of the inner powers accessible within that form. Finally, the heroic nature of the inhabiting soul is drawn forth through action in crisis. In some ways the whole story recapitulates each individual lifetime from infancy to adulthood as well as the longer span of the multileveled pilgrimage of the soul.

The story, although not parallel to life in all respects, also presents an interesting dichotomy between the real and the unreal. Whenever our hero exists—is awake—in one world, he is asleep in the other, creating identity and values issues. In a similar way, each of us in waking consciousness in this world can forget, or at least be out of sync with, the subtle world—which is our true home.

In addition to progressing from the lowest expression of form and consciousness to the highest, each soul must at some point develop a self-reliance and self-directed approach to dealing with every type of situation or problem it may encounter. Each soul must have "passed through every elemental form of the phenomenal world of that Manvantara."

This game of life places each one, as William Bendix, a long-forgotten radio comedian, used to say, in a most "revolting predicament." How else can we develop an ability to discern right from wrong, the important from the unimportant, the better from the lesser, or the real from the unreal? Step by step this kind of understanding grows; each task accomplished increases our confidence and self empowerment; each challenge overcome creates new growth of capacities from within. From youth to old age, one of the most satisfying experiences of existence is the mastery of an ability or the sense of a job well done—especially when great difficulties have been overcome. In this process "each soul must have acquired individuality, first by natural impulse, and then by self-induced and self-devised efforts (checked by its Karma), thus ascending through all the degrees of intelligence, from the lowest to the highest Manas, from mineral and plant, up to the holiest archangel (Dhyani-Buddha). The pivotal doctrine of the Esoteric Philosophy admits no privileges or special gifts in man, save those won by his own Ego through personal effort and merit throughout a long series of metempsychoses and reincarnations."

In the midst of a struggle it can be extremely hard to remember that each difficulty is truly an opportunity to reach deep into ourselves and draw on and strengthen the best that is within us. But once we grasp this truth, we discover a kind of joy or exhilaration in each trial overcome. This joy is the experience of our true self gaining its own strength and shining through our consciousness. When this creation and growth from within happens we realize that even in the midst of difficulties we can have "fun."

As you consider your own pilgrimage, reflect back on past trials and tribulations. Think about times that you rose to the occasion beyond your normal capabilities, or, as the saying goes, created lemonade when life handed you nothing but lemons. This is the ultimate creative activity in the medium of consciousness.

Through this kind of self-exploration, you may gain the insight that allows you to answer in the affirmative to the question about life: "Are we having fun yet?" Self-unfoldment and creation within consciousness is the ultimate fun!

APPENIDX

AN AMAZING EXPERIENCE—MY NDE

BECAUSE ALL THESE articles come from my inner life, I thought it might be helpful to give an expanded explanation of what I term "my wake-up call," the result of a near-death experience (NDE). In 1968, when I was 27, a so-called simple overnight surgery resulted in a full month's stay in the hospital. I endured several days in a semicomatose state, hanging on the edge of death, and then more weeks in which several of my body systems had various failures. After a long convalescence, I gradually returned to health. Since that time, I have been blessed with a productive and full life.

My near-death experience occurred, not in the operating room, but as a culmination of the several days at the edge of death post-surgery. Psychic sensitivity was greatly heightened at this time, and I was able to slip in and out of physical consciousness at will. I preferred staying in the other-worldly state, but could be called back whenever necessary.

I add this bit of information because a remarkable pre-NDE event occurred. Some years ago prior to my NDE, I had developed a resentment against my mother who was truly a wonderful human being. The resentment occurred because of some of my willful decisions as a teenager. It seems nonsensical now in retrospect, but my stubbornness became a barrier of my own making between us. This manifested as an ongoing resentment and psychological distancing.

Upon learning of my dire circumstance, she made the 8-hour drive to the hospital and showed up in the doorway of my room. In my sensitized state, upon seeing her full essence, I forgave her, dropping all the former barriers. At that moment what might be described as a crystalline cage shattered like broken glass and opened my consciousness to an expanded sphere and some sort of angelic music of rejoicing. While this was a particularly personal experience, I share it in order to highlight the necessity and power of resolving the restrictions that we create for ourselves through any kind of anger or resentment. I have often wondered whether the completeness of the NDE that followed depended upon this event.

At a crisis point, in the wee hours of the third morning after the surgery went wrong, I found myself in the presence of the "Council of Light." The Council exhibited a unity of purpose, but a diversity of points of view as expressed in clearly understandable thoughts from different origins within the Light. There were no specific forms as such, but different foci within the Light. They were great beings, but received me as if they were my partners in the life process. There was a total sense of rightness and familiarity as I experienced their presence—certainly no sense of cowering or surprise. They were welcoming, supportive, and totally non-condemnatory as they guided me through my life review.

An interesting aspect of the review was its non-linearity. Instead of a linear time review of events, or a sense of watching a movie, a series of thematic holographic bubbles arose, each drawing from obscure reaches of time until it incorporated the wholeness of a theme. Wherever my consciousness was focused, all aspects of a particular theme were present at once in their totality. Themes included relationships with individuals, qualities of being, and capacities developed, or the lack thereof.

Shortcomings were relegated to things to be covered in future lives and successes were acknowledged as completions. Oddly enough, as imperfect as I was, it was acknowledged that I had accomplished all that was necessary for this life. As little as I had done, it was enough! I was quite young, rather spoiled, and oblivious to the problems that so many in the world face. Perhaps this existence had been designated as a time of rest or recovery. Who knows? One can never know from external appearances what anyone's assigned tasks are for a lifetime. It is important to be careful when thinking that we know what a life's purpose may have been or that we have any right to judge another's path.

After reviewing the potential results of my death, the Council gave me a choice. I could remain in this afterlife state or I could choose to return to the physical world. There was serious discussion about whether I had developed enough strength of being to face my new life with its new assignments. I would be entering a new phase for which I was unprepared. As I considered, I set my face toward the challenge of a new direction on the earth plane. The Council of Light was supportive but allowed me to make my own decision. They did, however, give a dire warning that "It will not be as easy as you have had it up to this point, and be aware that you are definitely lacking in coping skills and street knowledge."

As a parting gift, in order that I might retain some memory of this occurrence, they gave me a keyword—"OTHERS." This was the only instruction that I remember: the word reverberated in my mind as I returned through a dark tunnel. Its resonance carried with it the essence of my encounter as well as a keynote for my life in the future.

From that level I did not pay a lot of attention to the physical, but after being catapulted back to that broken body, I thought maybe I should have reconsidered. My body was still a wreck and

I wondered how I could even get up to walk, much less be of some use. Yet, my inner life was reeling. I was stuck with the same personality quirks that did not resonate with this new awareness.

It may be that the shock of the experience loosened my subconscious, but a wave of realizations and adjustments flooded my awareness in a confusing and disconcerting way. Gradually I was able to integrate some of my new realizations. Over time my outlook and approach to life totally changed. No longer complacent, I was catapulted into an intense quest for understanding, seeking out new ideas, meditating deeply on my own motives, and drastically changing my interactions with life. I would continue to make mistakes but would be able to cope with the consequences as a part of learning and growing. Death had no sting; the grave had no victory; life was an important game, a classroom; but life was to be lived with a fervent intensity. Nothing mattered, but everything mattered! In fact, my husband of many years attests to the fact that I was transformed in reactions and attitude. I was living within a different worldview. He affirms that he has experienced two different persons in the same body of his wife.

Early in my search for understanding I discovered the Theosophical Society and related writings which were most helpful in providing context and in understanding the implications of my NDE. Certainly, the important thing for everyone is to recognize ourselves as but one small, connected part of the cosmos, and to live for the benefit of all.

I would like to leave you with a beautiful description of the "beyond" from *Open Heart, Open Mind* by Thomas Keating. He expressed better than I can the atmosphere that I experienced.

> This presence is so immense, yet so humble; awe-inspiring yet so gentle; limitless, yet so intimate,

tender and personal. I know that I am known. Everything in my life is transparent in this Presence. It knows everything about me—all my weaknesses, brokenness, sinfulness—and still loves me infinitely. This Presence is healing, strengthening, refreshing—just by its Presence. It is nonjudgmental, self-giving, seeking no reward, boundless in compassion. It is like coming home to a place I should never have left, to an awareness that was somehow always there, but which I did not recognize.

ACKNOWLEDGMENTS

This publication would never have come into being without the encouragement by my husband David Bland. I am grateful as well for my many friends who expressed an interest in the project, including my neighbor Mike Iannelli, who pleaded with me to make these writings more publicly available. I am also indebted to my daughter Dana Cowlishaw for her superb editing skills and to Drew Stevens for his professionalism and enthusiasm in pulling it all together. Special thanks for the cover artwork go to Suzanne Hetzel (www.dragonflywatercolors.com). Last but not least, a big thank you for permission to reprint the articles goes to *Quest: Journal of the Theosophical Society*, a publication of the Theosophical Society in America (www.theosophical.org).

INDEX OF TITLES AND ISSUE DATES

The issue date in which each article appeared in *Quest: Journal of the Theosophical Society*, is listed in the second column.

Made in the USA
Columbia, SC
08 January 2024

30034531R00115